THE KNOCK

THE KNOCK

AN UNEXPECTED WAKE UP CALL

ANDREW DEGREGORIO

Printed in the United States of America

First Printing, 2020

ISBN-13: 978-1-949003-05-5 print edition
ISBN-13: 978-1-949003-06-2 ebook edition
ISBN-13: 978-1-949003-07-9 audio edition

Waterside Productions
2055 Oxford Ave
Cardiff, CA 92007
www.waterside.com

*To my beautiful love and inspiration Felicia Gualda.
Thank you for all the support, kindness, and wisdom
that you gift me every day. I love you.*

TABLE OF CONTENTS

ACKNOWLEDGEMENTS

I would like to acknowledge William and Gayle Gladstone for inviting me into your home and allowing this book writing process to take place. Thank you, William, for being the gateway and the guidance that helped bring my story to the world.

Thank you William, Gayle, and Felicia for holding beautiful alignment during this book writing.

To Lorraine DeLear for being an amazing mentor and warm light that guided me in reconnecting back to who I am. Your deep well of compassion continues to inspire me every day.

I would like to acknowledge Anna-Lisa Adelberg and all the teachers and staff of Luminous Awareness Institute for giving me a home and an amazing energetic playground to continue to awaken, heal, and grow in. Your fierce dedication to awakening humanity into open-hearted awareness has brought great change to this world already.

To my family, my mom Wanda DeGregorio, my brother Steven DeGregorio, Jr. and my father Steven DeGregorio, Sr. for being my biggest teachers this life. I love you.

Thank you Peter Cummings for all of your wisdom and for being a profound guide for me into integrated well-being.

To my amazing clients, who keep showing up and are committed to their own well-being. You all inspire me to continue to deepen my own work. I have learned so much from all of you.

To all my teachers and mentors who have dedicated their life to service and the liberation of humanity.

To all the masters and enlightened beings who are deeply dedicated to this path and to the awakening of all beings from suffering. Thank you for your strong commitment, ongoing support for humanity, and your dedication to bringing peace and joy to all beings throughout the cosmos.

Finally, I would like to acknowledge the loving and wise intelligence of this amazing universe that has continued to guide me and hold me in all that I do.

PUBLISHER'S NOTE

This is an unusual book. I met Andrew through other Waterside author clients who raved about the success they were having due in part to his coaching. I had never worked directly with a life coach, so I was not sure what to expect. My wife Gayle and I had recorded several books with other Waterside clients, so when it became clear that Andrew was interested in authoring a book about his life experiences and his coaching techniques, we decided that we would meet with Andrew for two hours a week and record our sessions to see if a book might be generated. The first several sessions were fascinating as Gayle and I experienced Andrew's unique abilities and techniques, which included his ability to communicate with non-local energies, lead communication exercises, and focus his energy on specific healing interventions, which addressed present and past traumas, both physical and emotional. We had never met anyone with quite the combination of unique talents and caring that we experienced working with Andrew.

When we reviewed the transcripts of those initial sessions, we realized that they were really just the background that the three of us needed to understand Andrew's language and goals for his book. None of those sessions is included in the book you are reading. Since we had decided to start over, we invited Andrew's partner Felicia to join in the sessions. Felicia and Andrew have been together for over a year, and Felicia has developed some nontraditional healing techniques through her own work and her ongoing work with Andrew. Like Gayle, she brought some centering to the sessions, so even though she rarely spoke, she was a participant in the book you are now reading.

As an anthropologist, author, editor, filmmaker, and publisher I have overseen the development of dozens of successful books. I have a sense of what general audiences need to understand and an ability to help advanced and esoteric authors such as Andrew direct their focus in ways that will enable general readers to understand what are sometimes sophisticated concepts. I believe I have been successful in guiding Andrew so that the experience for readers will be both entertaining and insightful. Andrew was reluctant in early sessions to share his personal story details, but as we developed this book, he came to realize how important it is for readers to understand the context of Andrew's own development.

Not everyone will be able to develop the unique skills that Andrew has developed. Not everyone will have the patience to become fully self-aware. Not everyone will have their life interrupted by a major life-threatening accident that removes them from their daily routines for six months or more. But everyone can benefit from examining Andrew's personal journey and the insights and techniques which he shares in this book. Andrew's goal is to reach as many people as possible so that they can benefit from what he has learned and experienced. His techniques are simple and easy to implement in your own life. We hope that you do and that in so doing you improve your life and the lives of those with whom you share this planet. We are living in a time of dramatic change. For those open to receiving his gifts, Andrew can be a wonderful catalyst for positive change for you and those you most cherish.

May all aspects of your life be joyous.

—William Gladstone

INTRODUCTION

After a near death experience and hitting bottom, I was lost and confused, feeling depressed and totally alone. I realized I was stuck living in continuous habits of suffering that I thought were the nature of life. I couldn't continue like that. I wanted off this crazy planet. I decided to take a stand and take back my power. I was not going to be a victim and let life push me around anymore. I could feel this was going to be a long climb out of a deep, dark hole. But I had to find the answer of why I was stuck in a reality that seemed to be filled with so much disappointment and never-ending cycles of suffering. I moved forward with no idea of what I was doing. I was not sure where to begin. I felt something wise guiding me to turn inward to learn all that I could about myself. A sense of courage welled up inside me, along with a willingness to fully commit to face all that I would find out about myself, without judgment. These ingredients grew into a reflective awareness that became a powerful ally and tool on my journey and eventually became the foundation of all that I do. I share with you now the beginnings of this journey.

—Andrew DeGregorio

CHAPTER ONE
LOST LIVING IN EVERYDAY MIND

ANDREW: My name is Andrew DeGregorio. I was born in Pawtucket, Rhode Island, in 1981. I grew up in a hardworking middle-class family on the edge of a tough neighborhood. Looking back, I always thought that life was pretty good back then. As a small child, I kept mostly to myself. I have a brother who is about two years older than I am. It seemed like he just loved to pick on me most of the time. He was really wild growing up, always keeping me on my toes. Most days I never knew what would happen next. My parents both worked long hours, which provided a lot of free time for my brother and me to get into lots of trouble. Most of my childhood, my father owned a jewelry designing company that he poured his heart into. It was a struggle for him to keep it going. My mom attended nursing school, eventually becoming a nurse working many hours trying to move us to a better area to live.

I had a big imagination growing up. Playing with anything I would find while exploring the world all around me. I loved making friends with animals and bugs and getting into all sorts of trouble with the neighborhood kids. I was close with two of my grandparents who were around most of my life. My father's dad from Italy, who we called Papa, was a little old Italian who was shaped like a peanut M&M who just loved his scotch. He would pick us up to bring us to their home in Connecticut. He would drive around yelling at everyone in Italian while swinging a huge Maglite flashlight around. I would just crack up in the back seat of his car.

We loved going on rides with Papa. My grandmother was always kind to me, but was strict. It was easy to get anything past my Papa, but not her. She was actually my Dad's stepmother. I've met my grandmother on my mom's side who was a big personality with a warm Polish laugh who would just make you smile. I never knew my mom's dad. She passed when I was young.

BILL: Did the Italian background of your grandparents have any influence on your home life growing up?

ANDREW: Pasta. My mom cooked a lot of pasta. Pasta for days. Easy to make it in bulk to last as "easy" left-overs through the week. My mom is actually Polish though. Rhode Island is also known for some really good seafood, so we ate a lot of that. There is some really great food in Rhode Island. One thing I really miss is the food.

BILL: You thought everything was normal growing up. What was your greatest joy?

ANDREW: When I reflect back on my greatest joy—I struggle with this question. Family parties were fun. Basically, I enjoyed being left alone with my imagination. That was where I found my joy. And I really just kept to myself in my imagination doing things by myself. I was into things like building computers and learning about software and online gaming, things like this. I liked pulling electronics apart to see what was going on inside creating these experiences on the outside. When I was really young, I would build worlds with Lincoln Logs, toy cars, and LEGO. I would build universes to get lost in by combining toys and anything else I could find together, creating all sorts of cool things. My brother seemed to take joy in destroying anything I built. My aunt told me stories about how my brother treated me when I was first born. He would wrap telephone cords around my neck and drag me around like he was walking a toy dog. My mom would have to chase him down and stop him. I was told he once unhinged my highchair causing me to drop out onto the floor smashing my face. My aunt still remembers my swollen lips from that experience. He tried to flush me down the toilet. My aunt shared with me that she remembers always seeing a new bruise or bump on my head every time we would visit her. These experiences were constant throughout my childhood. I guess he liked to be the center of attention back then. He wasn't really excited when I came along.

We grew up in a neighborhood that wasn't that safe. We both made the best of it. Had some friends we hung out with and shared kid adventures. We climbed trees and built forts on garage roofs. My brother was bullied a lot at school and in the neighborhood. There were more than a few times he was beat up badly in front of me by other kids. It felt like we both had to be on high alert at all times when out. There were a couple times my bike was stolen while I was riding it. Neighborhood kids would ride around in packs. One kid would peddle while another would ride on the spokes. This set up would make it easy for them to jump off the spokes and charge you, knock you out, or down to take your bike. This happened to me while riding a brand new bike that I just received as a birthday gift. There were times when my brother would be attacked while we were walking home from school. We grew up in a non-practicing Catholic family. We did have to attend catechism classes at night. There were a few times when I felt so helpless while watching my brother get beat down by these kids that would wait outside the church for kids to come out. I was two years younger and I couldn't do much. I was a small, scrappy kid, but I was really terrified when these older kids would attack him. I love my brother and I hated seeing this happen in front of me. I felt helpless and heartbroken. We had a tough time in that area. I felt like I was always looking over my shoulder every day for the possibility of another attack. That is how I felt most of my young life, at any moment I would be attacked again.

BILL: Seems like a lot of the torture by your brother was just displaced revenge. He couldn't get back at these kids, so he might as well take it out on you?

ANDREW: That's what it felt like. I had to deal with those kids and my brother. It was a struggle for me growing up. I wasn't safe in the neighborhood. I did not feel safe at home with him or at school.

BILL: Well, having shared a little bit of that insecurity as a young person, the positive silver lining, of course, is you are wary when you're out in the world, and the outer world doesn't seem quite as formidable, because what you've already experienced was worse.

ANDREW: I became hyper-aware in life; unknowingly I was always scanning my surroundings for safety. Staying alert. I got really good at reading environments and people.

BILL: This is important as we later get into how you developed some of your techniques for being aware and safe in the world. And one of the things I know, having worked with you, is that you have an acute awareness of the importance of feeling safe.

ANDREW: A felt sense of safety, I feel, is one of the main ingredients of integrated well-being and for true transformation of our core ruptures to occur, safety must be present. Without a felt embodied sense of safety, our system is in a protective defense not allowing the flow of new information to be received, integrated, and embodied into the world. What I found interesting was I had no idea that most of my life I wasn't feeling safe until I experienced letting in the feeling of safety. It's like a fish born into water has no idea it's in water until it's pulled out of the water. Once the fish is pulled out of the water, it experiences the contrast of no water. It can realize the water and see what it's been in its whole life. It's like I was born into water that held the experience that the world was not safe. It's all I knew. There was constant evidence of this all around me growing up. Through these experiences, my biology was stuck on a constant high alert survival mode. Being in this all the time, I just thought this was how life was. I lived on exhausting constant high alert, believing this all of my life, not ever fully trusting others, life, and the universe. Eventually, through self-reflection and honoring those early experiences, I realized these were false beliefs.

At home, my parents did the best they could with what they knew. My mom did most of the taking care of us. She worked a lot. They both were hard workers trying to create a better life and move us to a safer neighborhood. It was tough for them to be fully present with us with all they had going on with my brother and work. And we were both a handful. Babysitters couldn't handle us, especially couldn't handle my brother. One babysitter literally left us with a note telling my parents they would never ·return. My brother tortured me a lot throughout most of my life. Just about everyday he was around me. I always wished we could have been closer. He and my mom were also always in constant conflict. Eventually, he was forced out of the house. Was given a choice to join the Navy or live on the streets. After he left home, we had minimal contact over the years. After a long rough road he is now currently doing really well. He spontaneously began his own meditation practices that led him to start up a successful construction company. He is living a stable life with his beloved and being a loving father taking care of his two boys. A couple years back he reached out a day after I attended a weekend of training that involved forgiveness practices. He apologized for all that we went through. It was a huge surprise. He came up at the transformational training a day before he called. It was wild. I've forgiven him fully and care deeply about his well-being.

BILL: Were you athletic?

ANDREW: I was a tiny kid so I was not big into sports. I tried hard to keep up with other kids and could hold my own. I did have a lot of physical injuries growing up, which made it hard to play sports. I fell out of a tree, broke my foot. My brother slammed our front solid wood door on my pinky finger and cut the tip off. I was lucky they were able to sew it back on, but now it has a nice pointy feature to it. I used to punk kids at school by putting it into a pencil sharpener and pretend I sharpened it. They would all freak out. I also had many head injuries as well. I had a huge rock that my brother tossed up in the air land on my head. I ended up with many stitches with that one. I had a milk crate smashed into my forehead by another kid at a party and had some stitches there as well. At another kid's birthday, I somehow managed to get a kid's tooth lodged into the back of my skull and received my first experience with staples on that one. So, I had a lot of physical trauma growing up without the actual playing of many sports. Seemed like I was really just into the sport injuries.

BILL: For many people, athletics is a way of surviving and being accepted. Because if you're good in athletics, people often give you a pass.

ANDREW: That's true. I gained a skill set in something else. My wit. And my comedic timing. So that's what helped me connect with people and get by. I did enjoy listening to my father's record collection. I was more into good music than sports. I had some neighborhood friends. As I got older—like sixth, seventh, eighth grade—I started to branch out. In high school, I had established some close friends who I always hung out with.

My dad's business eventually failed, and my mom worked hard as a nurse to move us out of that neighborhood. Once we moved, I became close to some kids in my new neighborhood who went to my high school. I had a lot of friends, I was connected to many people in different groups. I seemed to fit in with all [of them]—[I was] kind of a shapeshifter in school. But I had a primary group of friends I always hung out with.

As we got older, in later high school years, we got into a lot of trouble. I had a lot of freedom throughout this time because my mom worked late hours as a nurse from 7:00 p.m. to 7:00 a.m., which allowed me to come and go as I pleased without her knowing. During that time, my brother was in and out of the house. He was arrested a few times, and they gave him an ultimatum. He had to go to the Navy or be homeless. My family struggled a lot with my brother. A lot of attention went to him, trying to figure things out with him. I was pretty much just on my own doing my own thing while my parents were trying to handle him. I started working young and saved up a little money to purchase my first car when I was seventeen. I remember everyone piling in my green Maxima, even in the trunk at times. We used to drive around with people in my trunk. It would be either Fat Tom or Norberg in the trunk. They would always fight with who had to go in that weekend. We would drive to clubs and parties on the weekends. It was fun and new for a while, then drugs and fights started to show up.

Eventually, local raves became popular where we would drink and some of my close friends started to experiment with drugs. Club drugs, like ecstasy and other harder drugs became really regular with them. Things got really bad for a while. Lots of fights breaking out wherever we would go. One night we were out at a party. A friend of mine from my group who would always start fights, got stabbed through his hand with a broken bottle. He was a big guy who just went off the rails all the time. We jumped in our car, and the guys that he started the fight with chased us. They chased us down side streets, eventually catching up and running us off the road at a high speed. We hit the curb, causing our tire to blow out. We were boxed in, so we all piled out of the car knowing we were going to have to defend ourselves. I could see we were out-numbered. When we all got out, one of them pulled out a gun from under the seat scattering us in all directions. I ran so fast until I almost passed out. There was a truck nearby that I slid under, pulling myself up closer to it to not be seen. They walked slowly and paused right near the truck I was hiding under. My heart was beating so fast, but I felt like everything was moving in slow motion. I thought they were going to kill me. I know they would have shot me because one of their guys got hurt during the fight. They never found us. I waited under the car for hours until I knew I was clear.

When we all met back at the car, they had smashed it up, broke all the windows, cut all the wires and seats. We pushed the limits everywhere we went. I hated it. I always tried to be the voice of reason. I tried to get them to realize what was going on, but none of them would listen. I could see some of them were really starting to get lost in that world. They were staying up all night partying at warehouse raves, getting into constant fights. At first, some of the parties were fun. High school kids being kids exploring the world together. Lots of girls and guys having a good time, but eventually it all got out of control. I watched a friend of mine lay on the floor almost overdosing at a warehouse party. After this frightening experience, I tried really hard to get them all to stop. None of them would listen. Eventually, I had to distance myself from all of my closest friends to avoid dangerous situations. I didn't want to do that, but I felt I had to. We were all once really close, like brothers. It was a tough decision that I had to disconnect from them all for my own well-being. The drugs took them over. I became isolated and didn't connect with them much after that. One of them died from an overdose at a really young age. A few got arrested, ended up in jail. These were kind, middle class kids. I mean, it's not that they came from bad families. And really, you'd be surprised when you hear their backgrounds and stories that this would happen to them.

All this happened before I was eighteen. I kept it all to myself, not wanting to involve my family with my life at the risk of disappointing them or adding to the chaos that was going on with my brother. Unfortunately, I became the one that they would lean on. My mom, especially, I felt labeled me as the "good boy." I hated that feeling. I felt a lot of pressure to live up to such an image while I was watching the damage my brother was doing at that time. It wasn't my thing to be the model son. My family was under a lot of pressure when my father's business failed. He had to file bankruptcy. I felt like I had to keep up the image of being good to not add to all the chaos that was going on in life at that time. I began contemplating college, but I didn't really make a decision. It was like I was numb from all these experiences I went through. I wasn't making my own decisions at that time, which is really interesting as I look back.

My mom had a lot of influence over my decisions. Pushing me to do what she thought was the best thing for me. I hadn't fully claimed my autonomy yet. I just felt back then that that was normal. I was in a place where I didn't care anymore. So I applied to a few colleges and ended up at USF in Tampa, Florida. It was great because I finally felt like I was escaping this nightmare. I remember the first day. I felt free from it all. It was just me alone that first night walking around this huge college campus in the dark looking for my dorm, no clue where I was. I felt lost, wondering what I was even doing there. A student finally asked me if they could help me out, showing me where my dorm was. I remember that first night of college alone in my concrete, tiny dorm room that looked like a prison cell questioning, what the hell am I doing? Why am I here? What's going on? I did eventually graduate with a finance degree and economics minor. Degrees that I never actually wanted and never used. Funny thing is I'm actually terrible at math. I wanted to get into acting. That was one of my dreams. I loved to perform. I spoke to a school advisor who swayed me into finance. They did not support what I was telling them I wanted to do. "It's a bad idea. Don't get into that. If you want success in life go into finance, go into business." I don't like math. This is not what I want to do. Finance? They're like, "Everything in your record points you need to be in finance." I felt really pressured into something I could care less about with this idea that I didn't want to fail in life. I was like whatever, okay. So I had to go back and relearn math, because I'd actually ignored math throughout high school. I was more interested in the beautiful girl sitting in front of me than paying attention in class. Most of us cheated in my high school during algebra class. We had one person who was really good at math that would pass around his test because our teacher would fall asleep during tests. Instead of algebra I learned how I could get lost in the green eyes of this girl in front of me. So, I had to go back and relearn high school algebra in college to get a finance degree that I never really wanted in the first place. So it's pretty wild that I even have a degree where a strong math foundation is needed.

Most of my college days, I was floating around in confusion trying to figure out what I was actually doing there. There was a lot of partying going on at this college. It seemed like this was the thing to do. There were tailgating parties. Football parties. It was a big school, like 30,000 or 40,000 students. It's like a city in itself. I met a lot of great people from all over the world. I had to have a few jobs to pay for everything.

I worked nights at the on-campus computer lab. I was also working with a college security transport service on campus called SafeTeam. We would pick up students at night and take them from places like the library to their dorms. Basically, I got to drive golf carts around campus at night with a partner. Eventually, I became one of the directors of that organization. I was always trying to figure out ways to make extra money. I would pick up side jobs and figure out ways to make extra money online. I was just kind of crafty. I made money selling online digital gaming merchandise when online gaming became popular.

I also figured out how to make money through affiliate marketing in its early stages. There was a new company that would pay you if you got clicks on an ad banner link. So I created a script for a program that would just click the link all day. It paid a penny per click. For a few months I'd get checks in the mail for like $300. I was always coming up with ways to be in multiple places at once. Trying to be efficient. This almost got me kicked out of college. During my designated time given to pick up my classes, I was stuck working. I got crafty and figured out how to modify that ad click program to pick up my classes online before anyone else to be sure I got into the ones I needed to move forward before that filled up. I had to find a way to not miss these essential classes or I would have to wait another semester to take them.

One day, I received an urgent call that I had to come into my college admin office. They wouldn't fully disclose why. This was an office no one I knew had ever heard of or had been called into. I met with this serious looking guy that dug into me with some strange questions. I felt like he was trying to get me to admit to doing something, saying vague things like "We know what you did…" I was like, I don't know what I did. What did I do? I remember feeling really nervous, like something was going on. And they said, "Did you read the terms of agreement, the terms of service on the website that we use to choose classes?" I just laughed and responded, "Does anyone actually read the 1000-page terms of service agreement on any website? I just click and move on with my life like most people. I've never read those things." So, this program I created was helping me out by picking up a class that I needed to graduate while I was off at work. Once they fill up, you have to wait until the following semester, which would have delayed my graduation date. I must have messed up a comma or put a decimal in the wrong place. According to their tech guys, the program was clicking like 25,000 times a minute or something.

It somehow caused their site to lock up and eventually crash, unknowingly causing problems for the entire student body. I felt bad, I just wanted to graduate on time. They allowed me to stay. Going forward, I could no longer pick my classes online. I had to go to this office and pick my classes while being supervised.

At that time, I also began serving at a restaurant as a waiter. It was terrible. I enjoyed the other servers. Hated the job. Was barely getting by. Was barely making enough to pay my rent. We had fun there though. I knew I had to get out of there. During one of my night shifts, a couple came into the restaurant. They were on a date and I remember I was having some fun interacting with them. We were having a good time, we're laughing, and I told her I could guess exactly what she was going to order and exactly what he was going to order. I knew, I was right. And she was really impressed by this. She was like, "You'd be great at sales. Here's my card." And I was like, "Okay, cool sounds good."

After a few weeks I called her up and I got an interview with the company. It was a telecommunications company that was affiliated with Time Warner. At that time, they were hiring for sales. She said I could make really good money out of college. I said okay, cool. And I did the interview. They said I'd start making 30 to $40,000. I quickly became one of their top sales reps. I made, I think, around $70,000 the first year. I was about twenty-three years old at this time.

BILL: And you were in Florida, where the cost of living isn't that high? That's really good money.

ANDREW: It was good money. I had no idea where it went though. Probably the parties. I was spending a lot of money trying to buy happiness at that time. I started going on trips, including trips to Las Vegas. I played a lot of poker back then. I did okay with that. I played some big games. Enjoyed the challenge of reading other players at the table. It was like a game of chess with a bit of luck. I wasn't good with money though. My windshield wipers weren't even working on my car. I wouldn't know where my money went.

BILL: See, you should have paid attention in those math classes.

ANDREW: I should have paid attention in those math classes.

BILL: You don't need math so much for business. But you do need it to manage your own money.

ANDREW: Or just pay someone who's good at math.

BILL: So, you're partying too much. And spending money randomly. What changes the pattern?

ANDREW: I went through a surgery that changed everything. When I was twenty-seven, I had surgery on my left shoulder to repair a small tear in my rotator. There had been ongoing pain in that shoulder since I was sixteen. My father lived in Sarasota, Florida at that time. He wasn't doing well after a lot of hardships hit him in life. Once he lost his company, he tried to recover but never fully did. My parents were still together, but they were distant at the time. He was living alone in Sarasota. She was in Rhode Island. The hospital where [I had] my surgery was about an hour away in Sarasota. I was still living in Tampa at that time. My then girlfriend drove me down to spend the night at my dad's place with him before I went off to surgery in the morning the next day. He seemed a little off, and he couldn't sleep. I also couldn't sleep at all that night, so we hung out. We watched some of his favorite movies through the night, then eventually I went to bed for a few hours. The next day he wished me good luck on my surgery and said he loved me. I headed to the hospital. During my surgery, when I came out, I felt like something was different in the world, something felt deeply wrong. I found out that my Dad had passed away when I was in surgery.

BILL: Whoa!

ANDREW: He died that night. He was only sixty-four. He died of a heart attack. When I left the hospital, I remember driving home with my then girlfriend. I felt something in my gut. The pit of my stomach, this feeling like something was deeply wrong. My dad was a very caring, loving, open hearted guy. You know, I remember looking at my girlfriend, I said to her, "My dad is dead."

BILL: You knew it.

ANDREW: I knew it. And she was like, "What are you talking about?" She was freaked out. I was panicking and was about to drive down while still out of it from the surgery. I had to convince her I was right. She finally drove down with me. I called my aunt on the drive down to check on him. When I arrived, she was there and wouldn't allow me to go in, confirming what I already knew was true. I collapsed to the ground exhausted from the surgery and shock. A couple weeks before, he was at the hospital. His feet were swollen. I felt like he had something going on with his heart. I took him to the hospital and I found out that they messed up on his medication. They wouldn't refill some of the pills he needed without proper permission from his Rhode Island doctor. He kept trying to get his medication and they sent him home. Said he was doing better. He was stable. When I got to him that night before my surgery, he seemed okay. We had a beautiful night watching movies together. We connected. It was really a blessing to see my dad the night before he passed away. I got a chance to just hang out with him, do what he loved. We watched *The Godfather*. He loved *The Godfather*. It just was really, really beautiful to have that one last night before he passed away. The date of my surgery was a huge blessing. It felt planned.

BILL: What had caused the rotator problem?

ANDREW: I don't know exactly when the injury occurred because I had a lot of physical injuries growing up. I always remember having problems sleeping on that left side. It was in constant pain. I saw some doctors with not much help. I finally decided surgery was the way to go.

BILL: So your dad dies. And you're only twenty-seven. What changes does that bring into your world?

ANDREW: I started to reflect on my current job. I was doing well financially, but I was miserable living in a cubicle. I would make Post-It artwork while taking mindless calls. I felt like it was a soul-sucking job. It was a telecommunications company. I was basically living in an ugly brown cubicle, selling internet, cable, and phone with a headset on my face, bored out of my mind. But, hey, I had medical insurance.

BILL: "...Everything you want for the rest of your life..."

ANDREW: Oh yeah, it was terrible. It was not fun. I felt really empty. When my dad passed, I hit a place that was just—something had to change. And at that time, I was outside of this job pursuing a side career with a small company I started as a music manager. I love music. I was into arts, I was into music, and I really appreciated people's abilities to bring through music and perform. It just really opened me up. Something about that was so special. So, I would see this amazing potential in these creative people and wanted to support them in their dreams. I began to figure out what that looked like. I started booking people around Tampa here and there. And I helped start a monthly show. It's still going. I was one of the founders of a pretty big event they have in Tampa known as Rock the Park. I was asked to be on the board of directors. I brought some people together to launch it. This guy, Joe I knew from that time and brought in, still runs it. This felt good. It felt like I actually left a kind of legacy there, which is really beautiful. It's still a really popular event in Tampa every month that, as of now, is still going on. It's been going for many years. It was really beautiful to help create that. So music was something I was really into. But I wasn't making money doing that. So, I had to keep a regular job.

BILL: When I met you, you were living in California. What precipitated the move from Florida to California? Or was there some place in between on the journey?

ANDREW: You know, it's interesting, I just always had this feeling I needed to come out here. Even when I was in college I heard amazing things about San Diego. Six years before I moved, I visited a good friend of mine who lived in San Diego. I fell in love with San Diego during that visit. I thought it was a beautiful, interesting place. So, I had this pull, a calling to come to San Diego. And it felt like it'd be a better place to pursue a career in music. So I came out to San Diego in 2011. My then girlfriend and I did find a place before we came out, found an apartment. However, at this time, my girlfriend and I broke up and we ended up living together as exes. And that was not fun. That was a nightmare.

BILL: Probably hard to date. Your ex is right there.

ANDREW: It was terrible. And she would go on dates and come home and tell me about it. That's something we all dream about, hearing the details of an ex's new dating experience. I had to get out of there but I didn't have enough money at the time, so I had to try to figure something out. I felt stuck and miserable.

BILL: How long did that last?

ANDREW: Too long. Nine months.

BILL: So, authentic suffering.

ANDREW: I had to get out of that environment. I took all the money that I had in my 401k from the job that I was at previously in Florida. It wasn't a lot. I was using that money to survive, escape the living situation, and figure things out. I was just doing small jobs out here while trying to get my music management company moving. Eventually, I had to do something. I was working with musicians, but that wasn't paying. Basically doing a lot of free work hoping for one of them to take off. I used the rest of the money I had to move out and get my own place.

Eventually, I ended up in another sales job because I was fed up with struggling. What I was trying to do on my own wasn't working. I was working hard trying to figure everything out, but it just didn't work. I had to do something. I began searching for a job that might feel at least a little fulfilling. I found a company that sold green building products, construction products, and I thought, "Oh, this would be something that gives back to the environment; I could make money and it feels good." Something I wouldn't mind selling, really different than what I once was selling. So, I interviewed and landed the job. The way the sales structure was in the company, I had to build up a pipeline. The second year I started making a lot more money. I began to sell a lot of their business accounts, so they were thinking about promoting me. There was a lot of struggle though within this company with the guy that ran it. He was really aggressive. I tried to stick out as long as I could by convincing myself it was going to get better. It never did.

Basically, the first thirty years of my life I was lost trying to convince myself it would get better. I was living in a strange world where insanity seemed normal. I was just floating around clueless, trying to figure it all out without a map or a manual. Survival was all I knew. Just get by and hope for something to change. Hope that some sort of happiness was around the corner. The harder I tried, the more unhappy I felt. It just seemed to get darker and darker as time went on.

CHAPTER TWO
AWAKE UP CALL

ANDREW: In 2014, a month before I turned thirty-three, I had a near-death experience. I had been working about two years in a new sales job, selling environmentally friendly products. I thought this was going to be a lifelong career for me. Eventually, I realized there was a lot of internal conflict at the company, many unhappy employees were afraid of one of the owners. He ran the sales department like a dictator, using fear tactics to improve sales. It wasn't quite the company that I expected it to be. They painted a picture of a fun, connected work environment. They had a ping pong table, they had a basketball court inside, they had all this amazing stuff, but you couldn't use it. You had to be at your desk aggressively selling or you would be punished. We were told get on the phones, and push through and sell hard, and that never felt good for me. I enjoyed connecting with my customers organically. I felt a job of aggressively selling, treating people as numbers wasn't ever going to be fulfilling. It didn't feel satisfying. During the summer of 2014 I began to contemplate an exit. I made a clear decision to stay for a while until I saved up enough money and felt financially stable enough to leave.

I had begun surfing a few years earlier. In August of 2014, I finally started catching waves. Once surfing began to click, it felt really good. I wasn't an avid surfer, but I was beginning to enjoy the whole experience. One day, I was out in the ocean in Pacific Beach, California. Waves were big for me that day. Further out behind me in the ocean I noticed there were these two guys off in the distance heading for each other on a wave. I could see that they were about to collide. I thought to myself, "Oh, these guys are about to collide and one could hit me, I needed to dive under the water, dive deep into the ocean to protect myself and wait for the wave to pass overhead." I did just that; dove into the ocean, and went under the water.

When I popped back up I was facing the shore thinking the wave had passed over me. Out of nowhere, I felt a smash into the back of my head. Next thing I knew, I was disorientated, underwater. One of the guys that collided didn't have a leash on his surfboard. The wave carried his board and it speared me in the back of the head. It hit my head so hard that my brain bounced against the front of my skull and then the back. I was knocked unconscious. I came to underwater to what felt like a flash or surge of electricity inside my body. I remember seeing spots around my eyes, and bright white light. It felt like an energy woke me from remaining unconscious when I was under the water, saving me from drowning. Still attached to my board with the leash around my foot I was able to pull myself up. I was drooping over my board.

A woman nearby could tell that something was wrong. I could barely faintly hear her muffled voice; she was yelling something to me, but I couldn't make out the exact words. She came over and she asked if everything was okay. I just muttered something about needing help. I couldn't really speak. Seeing I was in distress she took the leash of my board and towed me to shore. She was speaking to me, asking me if I was okay. Keeping me conscious. I was literally dazed and confused, physically, emotionally, and mentally. I remember looking in her eyes and she was looking at me with deep care and concern. She was an Australian woman, had an Australian accent. She saved my life. I never had a chance to thank her. I'm really grateful for this angel of a woman. She found me laying on my board and was able to pull me to shore.

Lifeguards were called, they came over, they were checking on me. The surfboard that hit me ended up on shore without his owner. He came to retrieve it and saw what happened. Some tried to stop him from running off, but he took off. I was bleeding from the back of my head where the surfboard had hit me. Eventually they called an ambulance and took me to the hospital. I was in and out of consciousness on that trip. I faintly remember the paramedic kept trying to keep me conscious. I was making jokes. Trying to make light of my situation. My girlfriend I was with at that time was concerned, I was trying to make the situation easy for her. I was more worried about her fear than about my own injuries. I was thinking, "I gotta make sure she's not afraid," because I could see that she was scared for my safety as they loaded me onto the stretcher. I thought I was okay. I didn't realize the severity of what had happened to me.

At the hospital, a CAT scan found that I had three bleeds on my brain. I had two in the front of my brain, and one in the back. The board hit me hard, and when my brain bounced off the front of my skull and the back of my skull it caused three subdural hematomas and a severe concussion. So, they had to keep me overnight to make sure my brain didn't swell. I had a traumatic brain injury—actually, three traumatic brain injuries. The severity set in when they said my brain was bleeding and it could swell. I started feeling fear, that I could actually die from this injury.

There were many hospital staff checking in on me non-stop throughout the night. I've been to hospitals many times throughout my life from many physical injuries. I've never had that much supervised care at a hospital. How much they were monitoring me indicated to me that it was more severe than I thought. I was afraid that I could die that night. They kept me up all night, making sure my brain didn't swell. To what I interpreted as the doctor's surprise the next day, the bleeds had shrunk to a size that was safe to be discharged, and I was able to leave.

Post-concussion syndrome became really apparent within two to three days after the accident. I thought I was free and clear. I was wrong. I actually ended up with insomnia for the first week. I was up for five days straight. I remember calling the doctor stressed out saying, "Hey, I can't sleep, I don't know what's happening." They had me come in to check up on me, they prescribed me all sorts of different pills. I went on short disability at the time. Doctors kept me out of work. The post-concussion symptoms grew in severity as time went on. I ended up having constant vertigo, some personality changes, a lot of severe pain, and nonstop migraines. Insomnia was ongoing as well. This started happening over the course of the first few weeks. It started becoming more and more severe as the weeks passed.

My girlfriend called my manager and let him know I wasn't able to return to work for a while. For a brief time, I even started losing the ability to speak clearly. At times there was something wrong going on with my speech. There were a lot of interesting, unexpected side effects, and eventually I was told it was post-concussion syndrome. Something I had never even heard of. For the first month it was pretty severe. After that, the main symptoms that kept going were pain, vertigo, and migraines. I kept getting nausea, had sporadic insomnia, things like that kept happening on and off. That was for about four months, ongoing. I was on disability for many months. I was under a lot of stress feeling really scared I may not fully recover from this.

My life got much worse before it got better. About a month into that injury, I received a letter from the company I was with. They fired me when I was on disability. Found out this is legal in California. I never was able to generate a financially stable situation and exit on my own time. I was one of their top sales reps so they had no real reason to let me go. The owner and I never fully got along. He always wanted me to aggressively sell and I wouldn't follow his commands, but still had a lot of success. He would always give me a hard time, but since I was a top rep he wouldn't let me go. This situation gave him a reason. He needed to fill my position.

I ended up losing my source of income. They also switched my health insurance, which became a huge nightmare when dealing with a brain injury. It felt like the whole medical system failed me. Western medicine failed me. There was nobody giving me proper support, I was just being prescribed anti-depressants [and] all sorts of pain pills without any real answers on what to do to get well. I wouldn't take half the things they prescribed to me, but they kept prescribing me all these things that felt so far off of what I actually needed. Nobody was giving me information on how to feel better. Just mainly pills. Nothing they were giving me was working. Actually I was getting worse.

Strange pill side effects were now being added to my injury symptoms. They gave me things like Xanax when I had insomnia? I had a brain injury. I mean, it doesn't seem like Xanax would be good for a brain injury. I'm not a doctor, and at that time I even knew that this was ridiculous. I felt very neglected, just tossed around from one doctor to the next, in a failing system that seemed designed to treat only my symptoms with all these colorful confusing pills.

Everything in my life was a mess. I was deeply frustrated and wanted to give up on it all. Then about four months in, around the new year, I hit a place where I was just deeply depressed. I felt lost, isolated and just fed up with everything. I began to reflect back on my entire life experience. During this reflection, I could see the truth about how miserable I had been. Stuck living in an unsafe world in nonstop fear and sadness. How disconnected and confused I had been. How lost I'd always felt. As I reflected on my life experiences that led me to this point, I could see there were these repeating themed experiences that were all so similar that constantly kept happening. Relationships seemed to begin and end the same way over and over again with deep pain. I could see I had a lot of deep heartbreak throughout my entire life. Experienced a lot of loss, a lot of death, I lost a lot of friends to addictions, to sickness and drifting away. I could see that no matter how hard I tried, I could never pull myself out of the hole. I felt so alone. I felt so sad and I felt really depressed and disconnected. Honestly, I really didn't want to be on this planet anymore. I deeply longed for relief.

It felt like a few months into the injury I was at a point where I was taking what the doctors gave me to stop feeling pain. It would all just numb me. I felt numb. Everything was numb, I had no emotion, I felt unsupported, and I was in a dark place where I didn't care if I lived or died. I was in an unfulfilling relationship living with my girlfriend at the time. She and I both were lost together. Like two separate islands with no clue how to truly connect. I had a small amount of disability coming in keeping me afloat financially. The money lasted for, if I recall, a few months after the accident. They put me on a long term disability because I wasn't getting better. Nothing was working. I spiraled deep into a dark depression, along with this traumatic brain injury, with all the ongoing post-concussion symptoms and pill side effects. I was told I also had PTSD from the accident.

BILL: So, feeling like the traditional medical community was not able, or didn't help you, what did you do?

ANDREW: I knew something had to change, something had to shift in my life. Going into the new year I could feel there was something I needed to do to shift my life out of this darkness. I didn't know what it was going to be. But I did feel like there was this—it felt like a calling, or something inside me that was like a beacon flashing a faint message, "know yourself." I love the movie *The Matrix*. Reminded me of the scene where Keanu Reeves goes to see the Oracle. She points him to the sign above her door that's in Latin, *temet nosce* meaning "know thyself." I remember thinking to myself, I must "know thyself" for the answers I need, but how? Somehow this getting to know myself is of great value, and understanding why my life seemed to be repeating pain and the same things over and over again just seemed really important. I needed to understand why I kept feeling like suffering was the only thing that I'd been experiencing.

I felt deeply that if I knew myself, somehow this was going to help me. So, I stopped doing. I just sat. I began sitting on my couch watching myself and thoughts. And reflecting on my life. Each day that passed, most of all I did was contemplation of my life, and I began to witness all my inner thoughts without judging them to learn all about how I think. I began to watch my thoughts with pure curiosity every day. Through watching, I began realizing the same fear-based thought patterns were repeating in the background of my mind all day creating my behaviors. Witnessing all the ways I viewed reality, eventually I could see that I had this conditioned perception of reality that things had to be hard, that you have to work hard for everything, that you have to suffer to get anywhere; no pain, no gain. I began to watch day in and day out. I watched without interfering. I started noticing that through watching and getting to know myself, somehow actually I started to feel a little bit better.

BILL: Your focused attention shifted from experiencing your confusion and misery to wanting to understand the origin of your confused misery. It gave you a purpose that was the beginning of lifting you out of the experience. The reason I comment on this is my other client Eckhart Tolle has described how he was confused and miserable and experiencing many of the emotions that you've described. There came a moment when he too wanted to end his life. He looked in the mirror, and at that moment he realized that the person who wanted to end his life wasn't the essence of who he was. And he started on his path of being the witness to himself, very much as you've described. For the people reading this book, this is the key moment. This is the beginning of the change. Though nothing dramatic happened in that moment, it is like the tiller that changes the direction of the sailboat. It's this very small change of focused attention away from trying to solve the immediate problem. What med should I take, what doctor should I see… to just, "how did I get here?" And so, it's like you have a puzzle to solve, and so, it gave you something to do that was not totally negative.

ANDREW: Absolutely. This experience grew into one of my important daily life navigation tools that I still use in every moment. Over time, self-awareness grew in strength like a muscle through this simple yet powerful exercise that is always available. A curious reflective awareness that grew in strength inside of me began a journey that I never could have imagined. By using this tool, I was able to reflect and watch my inner world passively without attaching any judgement to what I found, creating a new sense of freedom and self-wisdom. I knew that I had to take a stand and deeply face my inner self no matter what. I had to face everything that was in there. I noticed that for some reason this was the hardest thing that I've ever experienced. You would think seeing what was inside yourself would be easy. I couldn't believe that just sitting and reflecting would be this hard. So much resistance and these wild distractions just kept pounding me. Through perseverance, the distractions lost their power over me.

BILL: When you say hard, what are the elements that are hard? Because being beaten by your brother wasn't easy.

ANDREW: That was easy compared to this. As I was watching these thought patterns and began to dig into my inner world by just watching and witnessing myself, seeing all these different things within me, I was met with this strong inner resistance within myself. I could see that some of these patterns, behaviors, and pain signals were actually protectors. I felt like I was being lazy. Not doing enough in the world. Actual physical pain, discomforts and distractions kept showing up in my body and mind. These protectors of me were there since I was a child, keeping me safe when being overwhelmed would have been too much for me and my nervous system to process. There is an intelligence in us all that creates powerful adaptive safety strategies to support us in navigating a complex world that would otherwise be too much for young children to handle.

Some protectors and safety strategies would try to shut me down from feeling. Others would try to distract my attention away from my inner experience of pain. These intelligent protectors began preventing me from feeling some of the deep overwhelming emotions from whenever I felt unsafe in the world as a child. A young child can only handle so much energy and emotional overwhelm in our developing nervous systems and bodies. These protections and inner safety strategies are an intelligent way that our system keeps us from actually dying from overwhelming energy and emotional experiences that can hit us out of nowhere. They were doing the best they could to keep me from facing my suffering and have been doing that all of my life.

Once they are active, they can stay active, causing us to live in an overwhelmed state draining us of energy and well-being. Protectors and safety strategies need to be approached with no agenda, with love and compassion for them to finally move over, allowing our systems to open back up and begin to process our experiences. As an adult, I found they were stuck on. They were just trying to keep me safe thinking I was still a child. Unintentionally causing repeated life experiences by keeping emotional triggers unprocessed inside me. I was met with these protectors and conditioned resistance the deeper I went in, which tried to stop me from going even further and seeing what was in the depths of me. I knew though, I just knew I had to move forward with compassion and acceptance, had to face the things inside me that I thought were true, but were actually lies.

With the true intention of loving all I found within me, these protectors would slowly step aside allowing me to process old experiences with my current updated reality. I discovered that many of these false beliefs about myself had been given to me through reflections that I received from people and experiences in my life. I began to realize I had been unknowingly lying to myself. I was unknowingly living in a reality where I believed that I was a victim, that reality was against me, that the world was against me. That I was alone on this life journey and it wasn't safe to let anyone in. That I needed to do it all myself. That life was hard. I had to face that that was just not the Truth, that I was just confused. I was so confused and lost unknowingly in denial.

I remember the exact moment when it happened. I was sitting in a chair in my new studio apartment. [I had] separated from my girlfriend a few months after I began reflecting on my thoughts thinking she was a cause of some of my suffering. As I started feeling better, I blamed the relationship for some of my then current misery. That this person I was with was a big part of the problem, and the boss at the old job was the problem, and that list went on blaming everything outside of me for my suffering. I decided to break the apartment lease, move to a new place to start over fresh with the little money I had left. As I was sitting in a chair using my inner reflective awareness practice, observing passively, I had this spontaneous flash of insight. This cold chill came through my entire body. I felt like a ton of bricks dropped on me.

At that very moment, the realization that I am the problem happened. I am the cause of all the unnecessary suffering that was happening in my life. No matter where I go, there I am. I couldn't run away from me. I had been lying to myself more than I had even discovered. It was hidden under all that blame. Under this victim consciousness that I was stuck living in. I had no idea that I was lying to myself because I was given these lies that began at birth. Seeing my entire life through conditioned lenses not ever knowing anything else. Society gave me this name, gave me these stories, gave me these voices, this inner critic, these judgements, all these things that I started to realize were within me. I thought they were me, but they were all false.

But I was the one actually always keeping them going. Making them real. It was a monumental moment in my journey that took unwavering courage to get to. In this key moment, I could see the importance of me realizing I had to face these lies head on with kindness. No one could just tell me this, it wouldn't have had the same impact. I could not be told what these lies were, I had to realize it fully within me and see it all for myself for my liberation to begin. My own realizations couldn't ever be denied by me. Once I had a realization I could never go back. Could never be plugged back into that false reality of the belief. This was power, this was my key to unlock the door to freedom. Now I had to walk through it.

BILL: Though this may be hard, for the first time you were confronting that you were not a victim. If you read *Man's Search for Meaning*, in which you have the account of someone who is in a concentration camp, and how he found within the very limited scope of what was permissible in the concentration camp, to remove himself from feeling he was a victim. I think this is perhaps the key, ultimately, as we progress in this book, to the techniques that you've developed to stop feeling like a victim, and to feel, no matter what the circumstance is, each of us as individuals have the potential and the ability to step through our programming to become the master of our fate. Because it's when we are the master of our fate that life can return to a state of joy, because you're literally captaining your ship. You are not, "Oh, there's a storm, okay, I'm going to go to the Bahamas in a cove for a few weeks and let the storm pass, whatever it may be..." This is a key for everyone. Are we playing the role of a victim, or are we willing to look at reality in a slightly different way in which we take responsibility for everything going on in our world?

ANDREW: Yes, and for me an eventual center of calm and peace began to grow in my life. The more I would practice self-reflection, the more I rested into this space where the stress of everyday life, these storms and chaos, would float all around me without much impact. I identified more and more as the eye of the hurricane instead of being swept up into the storms. From here, I could remain calm, remain centered having a much greater impact on the reality all around me with less and less effort. This became my new way of being. Stabilizing this state of calm that everyone has access to through self-awareness just spontaneously starting to arise, dropping me deeper into Presence while resting awareness into the ever present Now. I was finally steering my ship. No longer to be pushed around by life. Life began to embrace me.

CHAPTER THREE
A LOUD NOD FROM THE UNIVERSE

NDREW: After this life-shifting realization that I am the problem, I felt empowered. In that moment I was ready to [take] action, to do more about the victim consciousness, but I was clueless on where to begin. I had no background in personal development, didn't know what personal development even looked like. All I knew was that something had to shift. I had now taken responsibility for the reality I was in, and I wanted to fully set myself free.

I began by taking a step and looking into self-love and learning to embrace myself. I figured this would be a good place to start. I have heard people say "learn to love yourself," so what better place to begin by forming a relationship with myself. I got to know myself and fall in love with myself. It was like I began to date this new person, but it was me. I had no idea what it would look like. I started doing all this reading and research like self-love was some science project. I was beginning to know myself through reflecting awareness, but how does one love the self? It seemed strange that one could actually love the self, like there are two selves, one self loving, and another self being loved.

BILL: And so readers can understand, you didn't have significant resources available to you at this time?

ANDREW: No. I didn't have many resources at all. I had the internet, which most have access to. I started reading and little bits of learning online here and there about non-attachment, personal development, and different Zen practices. Things like that. In March, I figured I would look into finding some support with this. Therapy was an approach I decided to use to learn more about myself and to let go of places in my life where I was really stuck. I went to a therapist who specialized in EMDR therapy. This was a very specific healing modality, a form of therapy that focused more on the body then talking about problems getting lost in stories forever.

Traditional therapy has some benefits, however, trauma is held in the body and the entire human system. We need ways to fully release the triggers and cellular memories that hold the trauma and deeply rooted false belief systems in place. EMDR is a simple method that uses hand-held devices or eye movement to activate the left and right hemispheres of the brain creating bilateral stimulation resulting in desensitizing trauma, reducing fear, and emotional triggers from the past that still negatively impact us.

Many of us are easily triggered these days, quick to defend ourselves to protect ourselves. These triggers are causing some of us to disconnect from our lives and creating unhealthy, unconscious behavior. Triggers are even being used against us when we are unconscious. They are used by media, social media to generate behavior from the collective. Forgiving this extended control and locating these triggers is a way to free ourselves from the triggers controlling us.

Triggers can be experiences and behaviors we take in through our filters that can set off unconscious memories or past traumas causing our bodies to believe we may be under threat, causing involuntary responses, destabilizing our sense of safety, and activating defenses impacting our well-being and everyday life. These triggers generate an energy charge of fear that can cause us stress and activate our fight or flight response. Triggers activate memory that can be held in the cells, subconscious, and the body's nervous system, which EMDR helps desensitize and reduce their charge and control over our lives, eventually letting them go, freeing us from unnecessary suffering. When thinking of a traumatic or just a scary experience, if you feel tension, fear, or stress, this is something that EMDR can support letting go of, allowing for greater well-being and less anxiety in everyday life.

Trauma is pervasive in our society. Humans are actually very sensitive beings and we can store many unknown events, and these past events may be unknowingly looping or waiting for an experience to trigger them into action. Without receiving and processing this properly, they may be impacting our everyday lives in ways of pain, unconscious self-sabotage, and disconnection from others.

I was blessed that a good friend introduced me to somebody who did this therapy work. I went to see her and she gave me a really good deal to help me out. At the time, I didn't realize what was actually happening with EMDR because I didn't know much about it. I was just open and ready to dive into this work. She explained it to me, but I didn't understand what she was talking about back then. I just wanted to feel even better, more empowered. And that's what happened. I began to feel even better from the EMDR sessions. EMDR combined with the self-reflection process supported deeper contact within myself. From my being with myself more fully, what began to arise from me naturally was this organic loving authentic embrace of all my experiences.

Over time, I began to naturally and authentically treat myself with more kindness. I realized how unkind I had been to myself most of my life. As I got to know myself more, I was building a loving relationship with all I was finding out about me. Self-love naturally developed without having to *do* love. My self-reflecting awareness daily session revealed to me that my inner talk was always putting me down. This inner critic protector would shame me if I didn't live up to its unreachable standards. This stream of negative self-talk would beat me up with negative words and feelings. It always made me feel like I wasn't doing enough. Pushing me harder in all areas of life. No matter what I did, it was never good enough or ever acknowledged. It would make me feel bad, meaning based on my current reality or my life, I wasn't where I wanted to be.

I could see these negative thought patterns directed at me in the background all day long. Telling myself I'm not good enough, I'm not doing enough… I didn't recognize that the inner talk was always there because it was so natural and normalized. Like a white noise that somewhere along the line I just got used to. It was a strange negative thought stream on repeat in the background all day long. I began to feel how this stressed my body and caused me great pain. I was out of work and living on disability. A little money was coming in, but I was still struggling to pay my bills, to cover everything. I was running out of money and running out of time because the disability, the amount that was coming in, wasn't enough to cover everything. Every month I was losing a lot of money fast.

BILL: You use the initials of this therapy. Explain a little bit more for readers who aren't familiar.

ANDREW: EMDR therapy is eye movement desensitization reprocessing. There are a few ways that a session is done. You can either use a device that you hold in your left hand, your right hand, and it will vibrate your left hand, and vibrate your right hand, which begins to activate the left and right hemispheres to desensitize some sort of traumatic event or trauma in the body while you recall events in life that stress you out. An example of this was the accident I had in the ocean caused PTSD. Or a car accident can leave a charge or information in your nervous system that might not have fully resolved, including childhood traumas, relationship traumas, break-ups, things like this where anxiety is built up, pain is built up, and fear is built up in the system. This supports the release of that.

It's a wonderful therapy that is simple to do and helps reduce anxiety in life. We need support like EMDR to release experiences that are stuck inside us. We think just putting them out of conscious memory does the trick, but it doesn't. Events from our past are still impacting our life and well-being today, even if we don't consciously think of them. They must be fully processed and released.

BILL: And you said that she gave you a good deal, but how often did you have to go and how much did she charge you? ANDREW: She charged me only thirty dollars a session. She is a really sweet woman who operates in Encinitas here in San Diego named Anne. She was really sweet to help me out with that. I was really lucky. I had just enough money to go twice a month.

BILL: Sixty dollars a month, I'm thinking there may be people reading this book who could benefit from this type of therapy.

ANDREW: I believe it supports coherence within left and right hemispheres and balances many of our internal functions of the body. It supports bringing you into the Now and out of the past while easefully releasing overwhelm and reducing triggers in everyday life. It is also great for anybody who has a traumatic brain injury.

BILL: Well, you don't need to have a traumatic brain injury to benefit, because one of the things that is important for readers to realize is many times when you're too much in one side of the brain, you're going to be less than whole. Almost by definition in terms of what the right brain does and the left brain does, most people are dominated by one or the other, but whatever you can do to create balance so that you're not too much in one direction or the other is probably going to have a positive impact on your life.

ANDREW: Absolutely. It increases well-being, overall well-being, in all areas of your life.

BILL: What was your first breakthrough in terms of ending the negative self-talk as your first act of kindness to yourself? Was there a pivotal moment?

ANDREW: The realization of this negative self-talk stream was definitely the first breakthrough. I had to see it before anything could be done about it. Discovering that this was going on unknowingly in the background was a big deal. I now had the power to end it with that knowledge. Shortly after a few sessions of EMDR therapy and my own ongoing daily inner work, I felt another uptick in my baseline of everyday well-being. I began recognizing that through shifting how I felt inside, there was a clear shift of what was happening outside of me in my everyday reality.

I started meeting new people; these new people organically began coming into my life. With my ongoing commitment to myself, I incrementally continued feeling much better. I wasn't doing much to try to change my external circumstance. My focus was mostly on my inner world. Dismantling old beliefs, deconstructing old conditioning little by little. My external reality began to shift on its own out of nowhere. I first found this strange that by focusing on shifting my inner world, seeing this therapist, and working on myself through my own self-reflection and newly developing life navigation tools, my external experiences began to change. This was exciting.

So, I dug deeper into my commitment to myself. I began rapidly consuming knowledge about mindfulness practices, reading about Zen practices and things like that, putting what I learned from them into everyday practical use. I started learning how to actually take care of myself with kindness and honor. My external reality began to shift faster as my internal reality shifted. I could clearly see how big of a reflection the external reality that I was living in was to my internal reality. This was a really big deal for me. I had been working so hard most of my life to change only my external world without much luck. Ignoring my inner world was a blind spot that I didn't even know was this important to creating the life I've always wanted.

Now as I started doing inner work and started feeling better, things started showing up in my life without much effort from me out of nowhere. Things started changing rapidly for the better. "My outer world is a reflection of my inner world." No one ever told me this. I learned about many concepts like this. Many other great people have come to this same realization. One practice I found really freeing was the practice of non-attachment. It seemed to accelerate well-being in my life. This practice was the letting go of attachments to objects and things I thought were important in the world. Attachments to possessions, to ideas and thoughts.

I started to learn that if I let these attachments to things go—these attachments were like little identities that I had attachments to that I thought were me. Like, I am my job. I am the amount I make. I am what I do. As I began letting go of attachments to these ideas and thoughts, I immediately started feeling even better. My self-worth was no longer tied to what I was lacking. But this was an internal process to let these things go, building self-awareness of my attachments through self-reflecting, giving me my power back, which enabled me to let go of these false identities that caused me unnecessary suffering.

You don't have to get rid of all your stuff to live in non-attachment. Also, there is a healthy human attachment system that bonds families together, which is important for our well-being. Non-attachment doesn't mean to not have feelings or possessions. I could have things without attachment to things, without false identities to things. When you're identified with anything, like a car for example, if something happens to the car you will feel like it directly impacts you, causing you to suffer. Identities are so common that they can be easily missed. Some people identify with their jobs, some with titles like mom or doctor. We are so much more than just these temporary identities. We can fully honor and play these roles like mom and doctor without identifying with them. We can fully enjoy what life has to offer, knowing all things are impermanent. I learned to honor what I have without attachment to it, living fully in the world without attachment causing unnecessary suffering. Attachment leads to suffering, that is something that has always been true.

BILL: It's very interesting, yesterday Rory McIlroy won the Player's Championship. He's a champion golfer, and he had a year without winning. People were questioning him, and he said his big breakthrough was separating Rory the golfer from Rory the person. And then when he was able to step away, not only did his life exhibit greater joy in every aspect, but his golf improved also, because, "Well, I had a bad day, that doesn't mean I'm a bad golfer, it doesn't mean my life is negative."

So, it's interesting that your experience coming from a low place at the time is just as valuable to someone who's coming from a very high place. This ability to let go and just accept the environment without feeling that the environment is all that matters I think is part of the unique gift that you were given by having to let go. In your case, you didn't really have much of a choice. But in terms of how other people can benefit, what's interesting, and the reason I emphasize it, is it doesn't matter if they're low on resources financially, it doesn't matter even if they're in a position as you were, where they don't have a job. You can start wherever you are on the journey back. And as we'll discover, as you continue explaining, what's really hopeful for readers is that the journey back is to a place you've never been before. And it's a better place.

ANDREW: Absolutely.

BILL: Discuss a little bit about when things started to turn around. When you started to end your negative self-talk, and you started to be kinder to yourself, what started happening in your outer world?

ANDREW: The negative talk stream kept going for a while. This habit, like all of our habits, has momentum. It's usually a process to shed them. If I tried to stop it, it would get worse. Resistance seems to just create more of what you don't want in some cases. I just watched it and learned all about what it was doing. Kept an eagle-eyed view on it at all times. It pulled the plug on its power over me. At times, it was trying to protect me in its own warped way. I realized this inner critic is or once was a mechanism of self-protection. Through self-compassion, awareness of it, and love, it finally began to shift. During this self-love discovery process combined with all the internal shifts that were occurring, it was so obvious that my internal world was mirroring my outer. There was so much proof of this as I became always aware of my inner states, and at the same time, what I was experiencing externally.

As new ways of being set in with new thoughts, I began attracting like-minded people into my field of experience who were talking about the same stuff that I had been discovering. Through these new friends, I started to get more involved with personal development events locally, met people who were talking about things like consciousness and these terms that I had never heard before. These were much more positive people than those with whom I had generally associated. Part of me wondered at times if they were faking this positivity because I was not used to it. Some may have, but not all. They had a different outlook on life. I began to really enjoy meeting all these new people.

One of the significant things that also started to show up in my life were "synchronicities", a term I later learned. Synchronicities were these ongoing coincidental events that started to happen, that started to lead me to more and more of these local consciousness communities, more of these people and situations that were so in line with what I was uncovering.

Here's an example of a synchronistic event. I would learn about a very specific term or personal development practice online that I wanted to look into, and that same day [would be] led to a place or to people who would know about this concept through these coincidences. I'd feel the urge to head out to a café where I would meet somebody who randomly began a conversation with me. They would bring up that very concept without me mentioning it and tell me about an event that I would enjoy with the concept theme. Then I would meet another person who had nothing to do with that person in a totally different location who would tell me about the same event. Then I would see a book or sign with the name of that event in the title all within a few hours. I would listen and go to the event with openness and curiosity. I met more and more amazing people who pointed me in all these new directions of learning about this work. The more I would listen, the more I was getting these signals that I must go to these places and these events. A synchronistic journeying began. I call them "my bread crumbs from the universe." These bread-crumbs started leading me to amazing situations and people, and my life began to quickly change externally through these synchronicities.

BILL: What's interesting is one person's random events are another person's synchronicities. It's telling that you had this internal change, because the Andrew pre-accident probably wouldn't have been open to seeing these as breadcrumbs leading in a direction. You would have just dismissed them as, "Ah, that's just a random coincidence. Big deal." And focus on some-thing else. But you were in a place where you were willing to consider that the universe is not random and that there was a purpose to it, and that that purpose was able to communicate itself through "random events," which in fact are not random.

And the concept of synchronicity I think has been best written about by Carl Jung, the German psychologist, and I encourage people to read more about nature's synchronicities because it's becoming a very popular concept in scientific circles. It was not studied by scientists previously. It's hard to study because of the nature of synchronicities, and there's a level on which something that's synchronistic to you cannot be replicated because somebody else's synchronicities are going to be different. So, from the perspective of traditional positivistic materialism, it's not an easy con-cept to study. But as we enter the world of quantum physics and start learning more about the true nature of reality, it is proving to be a concept that has tremendous influence on trying to discover the true nature of our universe.

ANDREW: I had an interesting synchronicity with a quote from Wayne Dyer. This quote deeply touched my heart on my journey. It eventually evolved into what I considered a loud nod from the universe that I was on the right track. Whenever I came across it, it gave me even more energy to keep going. His quote became an ongoing synchronistic event that would appear all around me. When I heard it or someone would say it, I paid attention to what was going on.

Throughout this time in my life, out of nowhere I kept hearing this quote, seeing it all around. It wasn't like I was looking for it, I didn't even read his stuff at that time, but out of nowhere mid-conversation, someone would mention it to me. I began to see or hear it a few times a day, and everywhere I went, this quote was around me. It was like something was trying to tell me something and it was yelling at me. I finally figured it out after I was gifted a candle at an event. When the wax burned down on these candles a positive message would appear on the inside of the glass. Through daily use of this gifted candle—it smelled really good—the wax burned down revealing this hidden message on the side of the glass. Staring up at me was this quote: "If you change the way you look at things, the things you look at change."

My jaw dropped in shock. The one candle I was given out of all those candles with so many possible quotes was this quote. When I saw the quote on this glass, chills shot through my body. Tears out of nowhere welled up in my eyes. I felt so excited. I was aware that something intelligent was telling me something, something important. It cared so much and wanted me to know. In that moment, I fully realized the truth about individual perception, that each one of us sees a different world through all the different filters that have generated through our unique experiences of life.

Depending on the filter you're looking through, you're going to see the world through the red glasses, or yellow glasses, or the glasses of pain and suffering. Once we remove the glasses of conditioning, we will see in every experience there's so much going on. If I'm looking through a filter of negativity, I'm going to find the negative aspects of an experience. Now, if I get rid of the filters, there's unlimited options that might be going on in each experience. There's a lot of positive aspects, there's a lot of beauty in the world. There's a lot of amazing things that are happening. Magic is all around us.

BILL: "If you change the way you look at things, the things you look at change." I think it's worth repeating this because it's very subtle. "If you change the way you look at things, the things you look at change." I mean, from a positivistic scientific perspective, "What are you talking about? Things are things, it's all going to be the same." But the reality is, it's the observer impact. It's the observer who creates the reality. Some philosophers literally believe this. I don't think we're going that far. But the observer certainly influences the reality.

If you change the way you look at things, you're going to look at different things. For example, many of us just look at things, "Well, is that useful to me or not useful to me?" And if you're only looking at things in the universe that are useful to you, you're not going to be paying that much attention to, "Oh, look at the color of the sky, look at the flower, look at the butterfly..." You believe there's no utility in them. But if you start taking a different perception of what you are internally, you start realizing that, "Oh, the butterfly, the color of the sky, they're pretty fantastic!" And you put yourself in a different state of mind. So, explicate a little bit how that occurred, because it's easy to talk about, but all of us are programmed and have a tendency to fall back into that which is familiar. So, two things: One, how did you navigate this change so that you did change the way you looked at things, and how have you been able to maintain and even increase this.

ANDREW: We could choose to only focus on the negative in the world, ignoring all of the beauty, all of magic in life. This is a real choice we all have. Focusing on what others are feeding us is extending our power, giving away control of how we feel to people with agendas. We don't have to avoid what's going on, we can fully acknowledge what's not right in the world using discernment, and we can shift our focus to what's working or how to improve it.

As I started this conscious shift of my own awareness, letting go of my filters, the things I started noticing in my life were what I had instead of focusing on what I lacked. I had a roof over my head, I had a bed, I had new friends, these new experiences, and something greater began to speak to me through amazing messages. I started feeling even better, and this thing that I didn't know was going to arise, which we call gratitude, started showing up naturally. I didn't have to do a gratitude practice. You can't practice gratitude, in my opinion. You can become available for gratitude to arise through the practice of shifting your attention or awareness to what's actually working in your life. The feelings of gratitude naturally arise when you shift the way you look at your reality.

The practice is a shift of awareness, and what we focus on matters. What you focus on grows, this is where your energy flows. With a simple shift, you can immediately start to feel better physically, mentally, emotionally with a quick shift of attention to what's working no matter where you are in life. You start having more energy, you start to have better interactions with the people around you who are more positive. You start to look at people who you had in your life in very different ways. Through this realization and putting it into practice, my relationship with my mom began to shift. I noticed conversational shifts between us. I started deepening my conversations with her. I understood her more. Normally, I would have a two-minute check-in conversation from time to time. I love her, I check in on her, she checks in on me. Up until that point, we didn't have long connected conversations.

After this shift in awareness set in, I noticed out of nowhere we had a conversation that was a half-hour long. I'd never had that with her before in the past. For us, this was different and it felt amazing. It felt good to have that conversation. A practice I began to develop was to see all things in reality as new and fresh. This is a Zen practice of approaching all experiences as new from the Beginner's Mind. I began removing my filters and looking at every aspect of reality fresh and new.

From there, magic started to happen. Synchronicity kicked up even more and I followed its lead. I started meeting even more amazing people. I met the transformational comedian Kyle Cease. We did a video together that I was in with some amazing people that we all created from a flow state without a script, and it had eight million views on Facebook and hundreds of thousands on YouTube. It went viral, and had been viral for, I think two years in a row back when this first came out. It's called "How Enlightened Families Argue," and people loved it. And we weren't even trying. Just enjoying. For the first time, I started seeing big life results from not trying. Being in this absolute moment created access to a flow state, and amazing people kept coming into my life because I was looking at the world through this unfiltered way without criticizing and without judgement, and each experience I had was always new.

Things became even more interesting as I continued on. I had to continue to reflect on my everyday experience with reflective awareness because old conditioned behaviors would start to try to sneak back in. I had to stay committed, alert and awake. Eventually those shifted. I had to continue to see the world through fresh eyes, and through non-judgement. I continued my reflecting awareness and embracing awareness of all that was arising within myself. I just sat and observed my thoughts with open curiosity. I realized the more I would observe, and the more I shifted my awareness to what's working, that gratitude would naturally arise, compassion for myself would naturally arise.

What people called "self-love" naturally started showing up. Through open curious observation, I was getting to know all these false things that I thought I was, and I was letting them go, shedding it all little by little. I was becoming much more integrated within myself. But there was still a sense that something was missing. I'd wake up in the morning and I would sit on the edge of my bed and not move at first for five minutes a day, and then for hours, until I felt a deep calling to some action. I only witnessed my thoughts and feelings without agenda. This is a practice I still do today. I always sit and watch with open, soft, agenda-less curiosity.

The practice has naturally evolved a bit and at times naturally stabilizes into a resting clear, vibrant, seamless, inner/outer empty contentless pure open state of awareness that is awake to all that is arising within and without, of the entire boundless field of pure knowing. And I don't do it in a way that's like, "I have to do it." I do it because it feels amazing to do, and it's really great to explore this quality of pure consciousness that we can all learn to shift our identity into. I always continued this practice daily. I sit on the edge of my bed just resting in pure direct experience until it opens to this Awake Awareness that permeates all. It developed incrementally from five minutes a day, to ten minutes, to a half hour. Eventually I started doing hours a day. It was up to three hours a day at one point, naturally, out of nowhere. I couldn't get enough of it. It was unbelievable and beyond words.

From that pure aware state there is an open focus to the entire reality in front of me with a localized, effortless, open focus on my entire body and system. A relaxed diffused focus of the whole field of experience in front of me and in me, with small redirecting nonjudgmental adjustments if I lost this quality of open, relaxed focus. It would shift and at times toggle between local focus in body and the outer open focus of room. Eventually that shifted, because I eventually had an experience that shifted my understanding of reality. I realized through this reflecting that something was still missing. For a while, life got much better. Then out of nowhere things got really hard.

I became aware of a place in my body and in my system. I would say that I could feel this deep, dark depression that was hidden inside me that I was witnessing, and it wouldn't just go away. It kept screaming for my attention. So, I had this intuitive sense that I had to feel it. I couldn't just watch it. It seemed to just loop over and over again. I wouldn't recommend doing it this way for anybody, because I didn't know at the time what to do. I remember at that point on my journey I was learning how to feel my experience. Not just watch it from this spacious reflecting awareness and not resisting it either.

I learned about not resisting your experience from an Eckhart Tolle book. What you resist persists. So, filled with intense fear I was like, "Okay. I'm just going to go into it, I can do this." And I remember going into it and I felt this deep, dark well of intense pain inside me. This was April of that year. I remember it was hard to handle by myself. Let me say it this way, when I went into it, it was excruciating, and I remember curling over on my bed, tears rolling out of me. I felt despair and pain. A void that caused me to scream and I rolled over onto my bed with tears pouring out of me. My heart felt like it was breaking open and I didn't get out of bed for three days straight. I thought I was going to die. I felt alone. I literally thought I was dying. I was just lying in my bed waiting to die, didn't want to talk to anybody.

I laid in my bed for three days in excruciating pain and deep sadness. Eventually this dark void I was lost in began to melt away. It must of been hiding down in my unconsciousness and through my work it came to the surface to be met with acceptance. I found out later I could have approached this experience in an easier way to get through it with support and ease. So, that's why I'm saying, I don't recommend going through something that shows up on this path like this by yourself, but what happened after that was a new level of feeling; I felt so much better than I had ever felt. I never felt this before in my life, the way I felt after that. I felt calm, I felt peaceful to a new depth. A deeper sense of well-being stayed with me each day. I felt really happy after this, after I went through that experience.

A very significant synchronicity started to knock on my door right after that dark experience melted away. I began hearing about this woman named Lorraine who I needed to go see. I remember at that time I heard about her from this guy, and I remember hearing my inner critic voice saying, "I'm not going to go see anybody else; I'm doing therapy work, I'm doing all this reading, I'm doing all this reflecting; I just laid in bed for three days, what else do I need to do? I don't need to do anything else." But I kept getting this synchronicity. It was loud. I'm hearing this woman's name from multiple people. I'm seeing her name on street signs. I couldn't get her out of my head. Something was happening that was so statistically impossible with these synchronicities that I just had to listen to them.

So, eventually I reached out to this woman. I scheduled whatever I was scheduling with her through text. I didn't know what I was doing, I just scheduled a meeting with her. And eventually I went to see her. Not a clue what she did, not a clue how much she cost, I just went to this woman's house and I parked out in front of her house and went, "What the hell am I doing? I don't even know what this woman does." And this turned out to be a life-changing experience, a moment that in a flash would forever transform all of my reality. This is where my life truly began.

CHAPTER FOUR
THE RAINA

ILL: Tell us a little bit about this incredible woman who synchronic-
ally appeared, or at least the breadcrumbs that led you to her, at this
critical moment.

ANDREW: In May of 2015, nine months after the near death accident,
my life shifted into a new direction. I was finally feeling better, connecting with new and interesting people, had amazing experiences, and for
the first time was starting to actually enjoy my life. As things continued
to improve, there was still a deep feeling inside of me that something
was missing. I kept attending therapy sessions, even when I felt better.
Stopping was not an option. I was fully committed to ongoing growth and
daily practices no matter how much better I felt. Looking back, I thought
all the work I was doing was considered a lot of inner work. Maybe at the
time for me, it was.

Compared to my later experiences, my commitment level was still
low and I wasn't doing as much as I thought. We have a lot we are up
against with social and individual condition. It takes a high level of commitment to liberation every day to reach freedom. Most people have no
idea how not free they really are. Forgiveness and awareness are the keys,
and I had just begun the real inner journey, and to me it felt like I was in
it for fifty years already. In reality, it was only a few months.

When I heard about this woman that I must go see, I didn't really feel
like I needed any more help because of this false idea that I was doing a

lot of inner work already. Seeing somebody else or doing any more inner work made no sense to me. I felt like things were great, but I did have this strong sense again, that something was still missing, and it got louder as I became well. The synchronicities with this woman's name got louder and louder. Her name is Lorraine, and for some reason, I kept getting the message that I just had to go see this Lorraine.

BILL: Tell us the entire journey of the breadcrumbs. What was the first breadcrumb to Raina?

ANDREW: I was at an event helping film a promotional video for a company. We were at this really beautiful home in La Jolla with many people enjoying the space. Some of the new people I connected with on my journey owned a company that would create personal growth experiences for people in support of transformation, connection, and fun. They invited me to join the organization and help out at the event. I was into standup comedy at the time. I had been performing and writing for a local comedy show for a couple years and they wanted to bring some humor to a video they were filming at the event. It was at this beautiful home in La Jolla. I was sharing my NDE story and the inner journey I was on with a really open guy who uses surfing as a transformational tool in support of people's inner growth. He was into personal development and seemed to be really interested in what I had to say. This was the first time I ever met him. I wasn't ever used to people actually being fully present listening to my stories.

After I told him about my experience being stuck in bed during that three-day dark depression and all my past relationship struggles, he brought up this woman who he felt would be great for me to go see. He said I should go meet this woman Lorraine who is really kind and does some interesting work that I might enjoy. He said she is able to hold a safe space to open up in. I had no idea what that meant, and it didn't sound like something I was really into. I met this guy right after that dark depression experience I went through, and doing any more inner work felt like too much.

I took her info just to be nice and said I would go. I could feel myself totally write his suggestion off. I put her number in my phone and just forgot about it. A few days later, I randomly ran into that same guy in a café.

He smiled at me asking out of nowhere if I had called Lorraine. Just being nice again, in an unauthentic way, I said I was going to set up a time to see her with no plan to. I never thought I would see him again, so why would it matter. Then a few days later, I ran into him again. This was ridiculous. He asked me again during a quick hello if I had seen Lorraine. I kept seeing this guy I had just met, out of nowhere, in these totally random places. I couldn't get away from him.

When I ended up running into him for a third time, he jokingly said I was becoming a synchronicity for him. That comment woke something up in me to pay more attention. He then asked me again for a third time if I had seen Lorraine. I felt annoyed with him for asking again. Why does this guy keep asking me if I went to see this Lorraine lady? This third run-in was at another event, and we hung out a little longer. He mentioned he felt like I should call her. Strange things started happening after that.

I remember driving home when I saw a sign with the name Lorraine. I heard the name Lorraine from many other people that same week. Seemed like everywhere I went I kept seeing her name and hearing the name Lorraine. It was so strange. It was like something was calling me to go meet this woman. I couldn't deny it anymore. There was something trying to get my attention. I could no longer continue to ignore it. It felt obvious that I had to go see Lorraine.

And then I did, I did go see Lorraine. She was in north San Diego. We scheduled a time by text message. I pulled up to her house thinking to myself, "What am I doing?" I thought I was kind of crazy. I was like, why am I here? I don't know how much this woman costs. I don't know what I'm doing. Is this therapy? What am I getting into? I was nervous walking in and she was walking out of her house with somebody. She had this huge bright smile on her face. She warmly told me to head on in.

She led me inside to a small room. I sat down in a chair by the window. It was this little office she had in her home. There was a small table in the office with tissues on it, a few strange looking statues, a treatment bed, and three chairs. I remember sitting there wondering, looking around the office, "What does she do? What am I doing here?" [I was] feeling really anxious about being in this place. She came in and sat down. She had kind eyes, and she looked at me. Then she asked, "What brought me in?" I responded, "I don't really know."

I started telling her about what I had been going through over the past nine months. I told her about my relationship heartbreaks. After about a five-minute fast-talking ramble about my life, she took off her glasses, looked me up and down. She began to slowly tell me a story about how we all come into this world. We have these parents or caregivers who are trying to do the best they can with what they know. No matter how good they are, they all mess up with us. I was looking at her still trying to figure out what she does, and I remember thinking to myself, "Okay, so this story sounds like it's going to be therapy work. Okay. She must be a therapist." I looked over at this tiny chair next to me. It looked like a child's chair. I'm feeling nervous just wondering what's about to happen this whole time scanning her room for hints.

After, she tells me how our caregivers make mistakes that can cause us to live in our protections and defensive strategies disconnected from the world. She then tells me that my system is currently a protected closed system. I looked at her with this blank stare. I had no idea what she was talking about. Then she told me that most people are asleep without them even knowing it. She gave me *The Matrix* movie analogy. It's like *The Matrix* with people asleep walking around thinking they are free, yet they have this conditioning since birth about the world. They have their stories about reality that they defend without question, they believe they have all these identities of who and what they are. That made sense to me. I remember thinking to myself, "I get what Lorraine's talking about. She's talking about *The Matrix*. I understand. I love that movie. She seems nice." But I guess I didn't really understand, because I was still asleep to the Truth at that moment.

She held up her hands in front of her. This was really interesting. She put her hand up, and she placed one hand over her other hand, and she explained how once in a while, people have an experience and they pop their head up, and they glimpse something going on up here. I was confused, still scanning her room for clues, thinking to myself that I have no idea what this woman is talking about. This is about eight minutes into this experience, and she said something like, "Do I want to know what it feels to be an open system and what it's like to be up here?"

And I remember having this sarcastic inner dialogue at that moment, saying to myself, "Like, okay Morpheus, yes," while staring at her while she waits for an answer. And just thinking things to myself like, "Yup, I'll take the red pill." It truly felt like that scene in *The Matrix* where Neo had a choice to see the truth or not. Seemed like she was giving me a choice. I looked directly into her eyes and I said "yes."

In that moment as I said yes, strangely, time began to slow down. Something started to happen to me within my body in my lower abdomen. I started to feel a strange sensation in that area. I freaked out. I had just said yes to this woman, and all of a sudden she's looking at me. I started to feel something inside me. This experience made no sense to me. As this sensation started to grow in intensity I remember fearfully saying to her, "Are you an angel? Are you an alien? What the hell are you?" I backed away in my chair from her because I started feeling this odd experience.

Then I heard deep within myself this kind inner voice speak to me, "Do not resist, surrender into it." From all these practices I'd been practicing with non-attachment, non-resistance, learning about Eckhart Tolle's teachings, and all these different amazing lessons about resistance, I intuitively knew what that voice was asking me to do in that moment. I trusted it. I surrendered my awareness into that sensation that was arising. It was deep terror. It was actually a tremendous amount of terror inside my body. The feeling I was feeling was terror in the bottom of my stomach. As soon as I surrendered into this feeling of terror, it began to dissolve. I felt something quickly rise up through my spine and body. Through my physical body, I felt another powerful sensation shoot up and out my spine through my head. Like electricity shooting out of me.

What happened after that is impossible to fully capture in words. I'm going to do my best to describe what occurred after this. Once I fully surrendered into this terror, something quickly moved up my entire spine and felt like it blasted out of the top of my head, and there was this explosion of myself into nowhere, and I was no longer there. The *I* that I knew disappeared into everything, feeling fully connected to everything everywhere in the universe. Immense beauty was all around. In that moment, as my self exploded, for the first time ever, I felt true Love. Love flooding my entire being. It was everywhere, all around me, and It was always there. This intense warm Love poured through every cell of my physical body. It was this vibrant radiant loving light. This energetic feeling of love nourishing every cell, every sense pouring in and through my being.

In that moment, I no longer existed, but somehow I did exist. I had these clear wisdom insights rapidly move through me, what I would best describe as downloads or realizations. Understanding that everything matters, and nothing matters. Understanding things about reality I have never understood before. Realizing in that moment we are all eternal. Death could never really come. My mind could not understand what this meant. The mind disappeared in that moment, totally empty. Laughter began pouring out of me. I think I laughed together with this kind woman Lorraine for what felt like an eternity, but was about ten to fifteen minutes.

We just laughed. All we did was laugh and nothing mattered. I just felt bathed in a Loving light that was always everywhere. Now, somehow, everything just made sense. After this explosion, my eyes were wide open in a joyful bliss. I was laughing. I just started laughing at everything. Lorraine was laughing with me. I couldn't stop laughing. It was a deep laughter with no fear left in my body, I could see everything was perfect as it is. I connected, I could feel—it was a literal feeling of everything. What she meant by this idea of closed system is that I had these false identities that I believed were real, or this false idea that I was separate from everything. These ideas were defended by survival safety strategies and protectors keeping it all in place without me knowing. That was an absolute illusion. What she was referring to as a closed system was a way my defenses protected me from deep pain, unknowingly keeping me closed off from everything through keeping these protections going. In that moment, the terror from my mistaken identities let go, I reconnected to everything in this universe, out of this universe, into this nothingness of beauty and love. This effortless grace set me free. I was whole. Always was, always will be. A new journey had just begun.

BILL: Let me step in for the readers because it's the whole nature of our human existence to develop ourselves as closed systems. It's our survival retreat mechanism for the body. It does limit us, obviously, from this more expansive, deeper reality in which we actually are part of the open system, which is everything. Which is why nothing and everything matters. But when you're in your closed system, some things matter, and some things don't.

It's not to scare readers into thinking that they have to be in their expansive awareness at all times and give up what they've worked so hard to achieve. Because in the closed system, that's really the nature of the human journey. You start as an infant, and you go to school and you accomplish something. You get a job and you have your family, and all these parts of your identity are part of your closed system. There's joy within the closed system.

But of course, what Lorraine was exposing you to was the fact that that's not all there is. And when Lorraine was saying, "Well, do you want to step up?" It's because it's a totally expansive, blissful level of experience which cannot be obtained if you limit yourself entirely to your closed system. But I think it's important that readers understand that we're not—you're not, and I don't think Lorraine would either—belittling the closed system, which is where most of us reside most of the time.

The reality is, if you're able to also be in the more expansive aware reality, your closed system reality will also be enhanced. Because as you said in an earlier chapter, you'll change the things you look at, and the way you look at them. The reality is that there is joy all around you all the time. Even when in your closed system. "Oh, no, he's my enemy," or "He's going to get me," or "She's done me wrong..." All that can be true within the closed system, but when you look at it from the perspective of the open system, "Oh, they are being a great actor in this play, oh boy, we're all in it together, this is really fun!"

ANDREW: I had the realization that I was never actually separate from it. I was always connected. I didn't even know that I was searching for this, and I consciously wasn't. The thing is, when I started this work, I just wanted to feel better. I didn't know I was going to be led to Lorraine. I didn't know that she would be a catalyst for that experience where this reconnection back to the whole would take place. I had no expectation to feel what I felt, and having these realizations that showered on me without a desire to know them. I wasn't looking for that.

I had found something I didn't know I was looking for. I felt complete and no questions felt appropriate. I remember walking out of her house in a state of bliss that lasted for two and a half months where the identity of what I thought I was no longer was even there. It was just a state of ongoing bliss. It was a literal state of bliss that was flowing through me. I could feel this conscious energy moving through my body that I had never felt before. I had a visceral sense I was walking in a hot tub of love everywhere, and I just wanted to tell everybody, but most people thought I was insane.

BILL: Eckhart Tolle explains that after his own enlightenment experience, he just went and sat in a park for six or nine months to observe what the world was like from this higher awareness. It sounds like you were pretty much doing the same, but you have a more outgoing personality than Eckhart, so you wanted to share with everyone, much to their frightened reaction.

ANDREW: I was running around wide eyed. I looked like I was on some sort of drug, and I wasn't. I was high on life. I had another interesting experience after I left Lorraine's. I went back home and I sat on my floor for twelve hours with this wide-eyed look on my face and this giant never ending smile. Strange things started happening. I heard these whispers all around me. I didn't know what they were or where they were coming from. I had no fear about it though. I started feeling energy and tingling circulating throughout my body.

In the background of my inner mind—the best way to describe this experience that started happening—I could see totally separate from me a feeling, a sense of my entire personality, that was totally separate from me. The identity I had up until the moment I met Lorraine was in the background. I could clearly see the entire personality ego structure and all I could do was love it. There was just love for it. Love for all the fear and confusion it had been given. It wasn't even me loving it; there was just love there embracing it. I could see my entire identity trying to tell me to go do things in the world.

All these ideas, all these thoughts. All the conditioning I thought I was, was no longer me, I was totally separate from it. It was just rising and falling in this empty space that I now was, while resting in infinite love. I found out later that people call this an empty spacious awareness state. I walked around clearly in that state for about nine months. Things became what I would consider very magical, and what most people would call very strange. And they did call me strange. A lot of different occurrences started happening that were way out there. My everyday personality was no longer in control of my life. It was totally separate from me. It was just being loved. It was actually not separate; it was more like within me and being held by love that was just flowing through me like a stream of ideas and thoughts. The personality was the part that was trying to tell people, that wanted to tell people about love that's everywhere. The personality tried, and people thought it was insane. Thought I was insane. They thought I was just some weird guy.

BILL: It's like a little kid who has discovered something new and just wants to share it with everyone.

ANDREW: Yes. I thought people would get excited about this love. No, they were not excited. A lot of people thought I was joining a cult. Some of my family questioned my sanity. They thought I was suicidal. It was the first time in my life I wasn't even close to suicide. I was embracing life, enjoying life.

BILL: When I had what the Yale psychiatrist called a psychic break, and I've written about this in my novel *The Twelve*, it was a very similar experience. In my case, because I was at Yale and I was motivated towards intellectual process, I was reading Alfred North Whitehead's book, *Modes of Thought* and I was relating it all to what he had positioned as the ultimate intellectual challenge, which would be "understanding understanding."

Through a set of occurrences, I unraveled that mystery, and I was totally ecstatic and wanted to share it with the world. I had the very same experience you had. I wasn't suicidal. I wasn't disturbed by anything in the environment. But I disturbed the environment, because that was not the way a Yale undergraduate was supposed to act. My behavior frightened people. When people are frightened, they don't want to think that they're insane so they prefer to label you insane.

I share that experience because it can be quite unnerving when people don't respond to you. Now, this is several years later, you have a greater balance with integrating this awareness in a way that you can share it selectively. Because what I learned and what I'm sure you learned is, you need to choose with whom you're going to share this because it's not going to help them if they're not prepared for this awareness. And it can, in fact, hurt. You were fortunate that no one was in a position where they could take you to a mental institution, but they probably would have if they could have.

ANDREW: That's true. And through that experience, I was living in this reality where everything mattered and nothing mattered at the same time. It was hard to maintain this balance and integration. I quickly became aware that not many people could accept what I was sharing with them. I didn't know what to do with it. This human personality side began to feel isolated, and I started questioning my sanity for a while because the breadcrumbs kicked up, experiences started getting stranger, and this energy and light, or this alchemy, started to occur within my body, where I'd wake up in these sweats where energy was pouring through me.

I started having spontaneous organized movements through my body that I couldn't explain. I started seeing things all around me. Energies and lights. I had a realization that everything was perfect, but my personality thought I was having a psychotic break at the same time. A new search had begun within me. I wanted to understand what was happening. For the first time in my life, I felt whole. I felt suffering didn't have an impact on me the way it used to. I was no longer stuck in unnecessary suffering. I could feel impulses in me. I felt sadness. I felt joy. I felt anger.

I had a greater sense of well-being overall, but the way I used to suffer where I felt this emptiness or this hole in my whole being was no longer there. I felt whole. A new search began, reality began to lead me to new information, to teachers, to people who had information and maps that could help me to put words to what was occurring. This became an unexpectedly long adventure, being led to different types of healers and very significant experiences that began to explain to me what actually occurred and what happened—not only from the experience with Lorraine, but prior to that. Because this didn't happen just with Lorraine. This was a profound experience, a key realization that I had. Lorraine was a catalyst. BILL: And had you not met Lorraine, I don't think the intensity or the timing would have been the same.

ANDREW: Absolutely.

BILL: And that's probably why the synchronicities were happening, because this was the woman that you needed to meet at that precise moment.

ANDREW: She was, and many other key figures started showing up in life like Lorraine. She's still in my life to this day as a mentor and teacher. I love her dearly. She is a wonderful woman who lives in compassionate service to this world.

BILL: As a mentor and teacher, for those of us who are curious, what does Lorraine identify herself as? Is she your teacher? Is she a healer? Is she a therapist? How does she present herself?

ANDREW: That's a good question. I have never asked her her title. I know she does integrative healing work, similar to the work that I do now. She acts as a teacher and a guide for many people. She has people who live with her and she trains on different levels of awareness. She blends the awakening path with the growing up path. I've learned through many teachers, including Lorraine, and through the work I did. I also attended a healing arts school that she helped create with another amazing teacher, Anna-Lisa.

Together they have been creating a lineage of awakening and growing up, like psychology and waking up work together. I didn't realize when I first started the work after the catalyst of the near-death experience, that's what I began to do. I began to wake up, what people call wake up. I was missing a lot of the growing up work, like ego development. Through that call of getting to know myself, I spontaneously began to blend awakening practices like self-reflecting awareness and therapy with personal development. Awakening practices and growing up practices began to lead me on a journey of reconnection to truth. Human development with spiritual development, and they eventually collide into that union and I was available for that experience I had with Lorraine.

After Lorraine, she actually goes by Raina, what started to arise in my life, the best way to describe this, is that this conditioned response, this personality, was no longer in charge of my everyday experience. It would come back from time to time but would continue to drop away. The more I got out of the way, the more I was being led by life. No longer fighting this flow of life. Life was leading me, and it led me to significant experiences. For example, in Australia I met another amazing healer, and I had an extraordinary experience with him. He goes by the name the Love King—which back then, again, if I would have heard this guy's name before the experience, I would be going, "What the hell is a Love King?"

BILL: We will get to him in a future chapter. But to finish the chapter here, Lorraine, Raina, how was she interacting with you during this period of transition? Was she aware of what your journey was?

ANDREW: Strangely enough, she was just—this is why it's hard for me to put this to words—I remember going back to her and it wasn't quite the same experience I had had. We did a session like we did the last time, but it was more like she gave me some insight, some guidance of what to look for, of what occurred, and she told me about the beginning of the school that was going to start in about six to nine months. She suggested that I should look into that. With what little money I had left, I flew up to an event that they were putting on to enroll people into the school.

I spent the last of my money at that time to go up to this event to figure out what had happened to me. It was in Northern California at a Zen center in Muir Beach. I went to this event, but did not get my answer because there was a lot more to do before I could embody this fully. Strangely enough, there was no urge to ask Raina what had happened. Everything became a guidance that I started following. Here's a way I try to explain this. I remember telling people about that experience, I was telling people about Lorraine and they went to her, and they didn't have the same experience. They thought she was absolutely amazing, but that they didn't have this explosive experience I had had. That's when I realized something interesting occurred with me that others were not experiencing. I was confused by that. I wanted everybody to feel the love. I wanted everybody to have that experience. I thought she was the person to go to for that love experience. I was wrong.

BILL: What's interesting from my semi-objective vantage point, is the experience you had with Raina was closer to what I and many other people who have had near-death experiences, have experienced. You didn't actually have that experience in your actual near-death. Your actual near-death experience for you was just trauma.

ANDREW: That's right.

BILL: And this is kind of the good part of a near-death experience, delayed nine months later.

ANDREW: That's right.

BILL: Almost as if it had to be born.

ANDREW: That's exactly right. It was like I was being led through a process that eventually led me to her. As I stuck with that reflective awareness and mindfulness practices, I began to let go of my personality identity. My relationship with reality unknowingly shifted. I started to listen to reality and reality led me to this woman, to this experience.

BILL: One of the positive things for readers is it shows that you don't need to have the traumatic part of the near-death experience to have the positive experience that you had with Raina. And how each individual who is interested in, as Raina said, rising to that level, achieves that experience is going to be individual. And that's why not everyone who goes to Raina has that experience, because I think it probably had more to do in your case with the emptying that you did. You completely emptied yourself and you arrived in a place of non-attachment.

So, you didn't have any mission other than, well, the universe is telling me to see this woman, I better go see her. And then letting whatever could happen, happen. Whereas if someone would have gone there with specific issues, "I'm having trouble in my marriage," or "I'm having trouble with my kids," or "I'm having trouble at work," they probably would have had a great experience, but it would have been more limited in terms of helping them deal with those specific issues.

ANDREW: That's exactly right. I arrived with no expectation, and the only thing that was there within me was curiosity: "Why am I here?" You're right about the emptying, because for many months I was emptying and doing my work, reflective awareness, embracing myself and letting go, and in that moment with Raina, literally just let go.

So, the thing that Raina reflected to me was that there was still a part within me that was in terror, still holding on to a false idea that I didn't know in the subconscious or unconscious, and when that blasted through me, that experience naturally started to show up. It wasn't because of Raina; she was a catalyst. I didn't do anything; she didn't do anything. It was a grace that appeared in my life through—I don't know if it was timing or divine timing—but through doing the inner work and letting go, it got me prepared to receive this blessing. I had let go of all these false ideas and things I thought I needed to have a realization of what I actually am.

BILL: It's also the terror followed by the bliss. What is common, whether you're talking about Joseph Campbell and the hero's journey, there seems to be, and it's probably beyond just the human experience, but for the moment we'll limit it to the human experience, where there is a need to overcome, whether you want to call it negative dark challenges, but there's a need to transform and it often comes with a certain degree of hardship or trauma. Somehow, without that, it's rare to then have the bliss, total awareness experience. I think this is something that can be very reassuring. You don't need to go out and seek any negativity. There's an abundance of negativity in the world. Some is probably going to fall on most of us. But the good news is, when it does, we might be able to maintain greater equilibrium by realizing that it may be the very negative that is happening to us that has within it the hidden gem that we would not otherwise uncover. Because that seems to be the case that you experienced on multiple levels.

ANDREW: As you share that, it reminds me of one of the realizations I had over these years that we are now at a time where, as humans, we don't have to suffer to have these realizations anymore. That was an old path of suffering and sacrifice. If we don't begin to listen to our internal intuition and we continue to ignore ourselves, we will suffer, and we can get forced into this path. You can go kicking and screaming, or you can go with the flow. You can begin to move toward the path of wisdom and begin to actively listen to your inner guidance and your truth, and you can have your own realizations without suffering. So humanity is in a whole new place.

BILL: Also, because of technology, unfortunately, vicariously you can have all the suffering you want without needing to experience it personally. So, we are in a different place in time. Now Barbara Marx Hubbard believes in conscious evolution, that we're consciously evolving, and that this is a unique moment in the history of the world because of the interconnectedness.

The individual is at a place today, when you're in an enlightened state as you achieved with the catalyst of Raina, you're actually in a place that is beyond anything that, if you accept historical figures such as Buddha or Jesus or Mohammed, or any enlightened, blissed-out being, you're actually at a level—because of the inner-connectedness of the collective consciousness of which you are both a representation and a part—at a level that has never before existed on this earth. Whether you want to give that any special value or not is totally up to you as the reader, but it is undeniably an opportunity for those who are on a spiritual path to realize that these are simultaneously perhaps the worst of times and the best of times. Because of the trauma that the planet is experiencing, particularly the human element of the planet, there is also, for the first time ever in human history, opportunity to reach enlightenment at a level which is more embracing of the collective nature of consciousness than has ever existed before.

ANDREW: Many beautiful, loving masters have come before us. They have laid the groundwork by setting grooves in consciousness that make it even easier for humanity to return back to the truth. With the intention to know ourselves fully, to be the change in the world through our own inner exploration and to return back to our open-hearted awareness, we can live in The Kingdom that is promised to us all. It is for everyone. There are no damned. There is no one lost unless they choose to be lost. We have been blessed with amazing way showers, beings that care deeply about humanity's well-being. It is an individual choice. No one can do it for us. We must be committed, and with that authentic commitment we will be led. We will return back to love.

CHAPTER FIVE

THE LOVE KING

A NDREW: After the experience I had with Raina, a new search began to arise inside of me. I felt called to understand what was going on, what actually happened during this experience with Raina. Something new was arising out of me that I had no language for. I began following this upgraded operating system inside of me that I now call Awake Alignment. Awake Alignment rapidly led me to many more new experiences, new people, and pieces to this puzzle that started to reveal a picture of what was going on. One of those calls eventually led me to Sydney, Australia. I had this calling inside. An inner knowing of truth that I needed to go to Sydney. I had never left the United States before this.

I ended up buying a ticket and went to visit a good buddy of mine who was staying in Sydney. On the plane ride flying over to Sydney, I ended up sitting next to someone who was one of Britney Spears's backup dancers. This person was really intriguing. During our conversation, he talked about healing work, energy work. He talked about consciousness. Before I started this work, I had never talked to anybody random about healing or consciousness. But all of the sudden, everywhere I went I was bumping into people, really interesting people, who were talking about these consciousness practices and ways of being in life that I had never experienced. Everywhere I'd go, I'd meet somebody who was doing some kind of cool healing work or personal development work as I was following this new navigation system within me.

BILL: Talk a little bit about the motivation to fly to Australia, because you're still at a place where you have very limited financial resources, so this was a big decision, flying to Australia, even if you get a fly-by-night airline.

ANDREW: Yes. I ended up having some points on a credit card, so I used those for a free flight. It was still too expensive for me at that time. I had to trust.

BILL: Which is my point, because it's not so much about expensive/not expensive, but for you, you had to have some significant motivation. You had never left the country before, you were not really financially stable, so what was the motivation?

ANDREW: The truth is that inside me I had this feeling I had to go. Like with Raina, I kept hearing this information that I had to go meet her. It got louder. The voice or the intuition, or this calling inside me basically got much louder, and when I felt into it, when I thought about going off to Australia, I would get body chills, a phenomenon I never had experienced before. The hairs on my arm would actually stand up. I felt energy flowing through my arms when I heard of Sydney or thought of it. I didn't know how to explain it, but this made it clear I had to follow this message.

BILL: It's more like we discussed before with the bread crumbs and the synchronicities, and you're beginning to look at life as unfolding in front of you rather than you planning it. So my question is, how did the universe attract you toward Australia? Because as we're about to learn, something very significant happened.

ANDREW: I had a feeling inside of me. I just had to go there. There was no other way to describe this, that I just knew I had to go. When I thought of it, I got chills. I felt excited. My buddy had a place in Sydney and he was doing business there, so I was able to stay with him at no cost. I was able to get the cost for the trip down overall. The interesting thing was, I could see my personality was stressed out by this. I could actually see and hear myself, witnessing myself with all these fearful thoughts coming and going inside of me. And again, it sounds strange, because I'm talking about myself, but I could see this and it didn't quite have an impact on me like it used to, because I would have never gone. Fear was there, but fear was no longer in full control of my life. I would have never bought this ticket or made this decision to go if the old small self was in charge. As I started coming closer and closer to the trip, more and more I transcended my small self and listened to that feeling arising from my inner being, and it just seemed to be the thing that led me to amazing experiences, so I began to trust that inner voice. Everything lined up easily to make it happen.

BILL: So, you get off the plane in Australia, and where do you go?

ANDREW: Well, breakfast. And I'll tell you, just a side note, breakfast in Australia in Sydney is amazing. I had never had breakfast like that before. It changed my life when it comes to breakfast. I couldn't believe it. Spoiled. They really know how to do breakfast out there. They call it brekkie. So good. Amazing, amazing. Besides the experience I had with the Love King, that we're going to get into, the breakfast was top notch, and those people are beautiful in Australia as well. I don't know what they're feeding them out there, but everyone is like a model in Australia. Unbelievable place. I really enjoyed Sydney. The highlight, though, was a few days later.

I'm out with my buddy, he's showing me around, we're going to these different places. About four or five days into the trip, and we're just walking for hours, miles and miles of walking, showing me all around Sydney. I remember getting this feeling that we had to go down a particular street. It was a pull, a magnetic pull, within me that we had to go, this very specific street. I don't remember the name of it, but I remember we had to go down there. There were some small shops all around. I stood in front of this small, strange-looking shop, and I knew, "I gotta go in here." And when I went in, it was this place filled with crystals, strange little statues, little gods, deities and things like that, and this is the first time I ever experienced a shop like this. My buddy I was with, I could tell he felt a little uncomfortable. He said, "I got to go outside and smoke a cigarette." He seemed stressed out by the shop and needed to escape; and I oddly felt quite at home.

I remember speaking to the woman who was in charge of the shop, and we had made interesting eye contact before we spoke, and I could feel she could see me a certain way, and I could truly see her. It was like we were floating above the collective. And we knew it. She was looking at me, and I was looking at her for a long time, and I could feel there was something interesting going on in this place. It had a very mysterious vibe. It was really intriguing. Her husband came out and I looked at him, and I could see his eyes had this glow to them.

I asked his wife about what they did here. She told me that he was a healer and that he did healing work. Remember I spoke about those chills. I could feel chills moving through my entire body when she said this. I knew instantly I had to do something with this guy. So with some of the money I had left for the trip, I booked a session, and I had to come back the next day. My buddy thought I was crazy, but I got in a cab the next day and went back to the shop. I thought to myself that I didn't have a phone. I didn't have much money with me. I went in, met with him in the shop area.

With his shiny, glowing eyes, he led me down this dark damp hallway, through all these interesting back rooms filled with strange wigs, down these dark stairs into this basement. I'm looking around. I hear in the background this really loud sound, it sounded like when you have shoes spinning in a dryer, like a banging. And I'm thinking, "What is this loud sound?" I'm continuing looking around at all these odd-looking things. There's strange, large candles burning everywhere. Odd smells of smoky burning incense. This cave-like feel that is dimly lit. There are strange smells shifting as we passed through room to room. Interesting décor draped on all of the walls. Masks and there's also wigs of all kinds hanging on these stone walls.

This is a very strange experience, a strange place that in the past I would have never went into. I could hear within me that my personality and my inner voice are in dialogue, "What the hell are you doing? Why are you here right now? This doesn't make sense; you don't have a phone, you're in this deep dimly lit basement with this guy who is quite big. Much bigger than you. There is creepy hair hanging up everywhere." And he comes over and stands next to me. He has a towel hanging down over his shoulder, and he starts touching my left arm around my shoulder at first feeling around not saying much.

As he feels around my shoulder, I'm just watching him with no idea what he's doing. Just wondering to myself, "What lucky person is going to be wearing my hair as a wig next week?" Eventually, after a while of him poking around, he begins telling me that I have stuck emotion in my left arm and shoulder. I'm thinking "Okay. Stuck emotion. Cool. Lets unstick this emotion." This is the first time I ever heard about stuck emotion in the body. I had no idea what he meant by this, but I was intrigued. He goes on telling me it has to do with relationships, with women or the mother line of my family, and it's the left side of my body. He's telling me all this stuff about the left side of the body that has to do with the feminine energies. I'm just trying to keep up with him wondering how he plans on unsticking that emotion. I'm also looking around this dark room and I'm becoming more intrigued by the surroundings than what he's saying.

He also said he saw chains on my wrist. He's telling me about a past life experience. Again, I had never heard anything like this before. I was thinking, "Okay, cool past life experiences. What do we do about those chains?" He then turned his head, and as he's lightly pushing my left shoulder, with a towel hanging on his arm like a waiter at a restaurant, he turns his head, and he begins to scream, "Roarrr!" He just yells like a lion out of nowhere. All I could do was start laughing at this. I couldn't help it. I just started cracking up. I thought this was hilarious. I could hear my inner critic voice saying, "This guy is going to eat you! Get the hell out of here! What are you doing? Why are you here? This makes no sense. You're going to die right now." And there's the comedian part of me, I could hear my comedian side in this inner voice dialogue thinking, "This is great material; do not forget to write this down." Because I did stand-up comedy for a few years, I had the habit of always looking for new material. That part of me was thinking, this is going to be hilarious.

Without any response to my laughter he turns his head again, lets out another load roar, and all of a sudden I felt a fire rise up through me. The best way to describe it, it was like this fire energy filled with love shoots up through my whole body and out my arms, out my legs, and this energy, or this fiery feeling was moving through my whole body, and I didn't laugh anymore. I was just in shock. Stunned. In awe. This felt amazing. Whatever came through me when this guy screamed made him cry.

Because he's wiping tears out of his eyes with that towel. And he does it again and more tears. Saying "there's the stuck emotion". He's wiping more tears from his eyes. And then he goes through these different techniques on my entire body for over an hour. He's screaming out what he said was stuck emotion that was trapped in my body causing me unnecessary pain. I took all that he said really seriously after experiencing that love fire he shot through me. I was in awe through the rest of that experience. I left after a little over an hour session with him, and that night was the first night since I was sixteen that I was able to sleep on my left arm. I had no more pain, no more problems in my left arm. The surgery when I was twenty-seven on my left arm had been ineffective. This guy screamed and fixed my arm. How could this be? He tells me it was stuck emotion. I had to learn about this. This Love King was the real deal.

BILL: Was he aboriginal?

ANDREW: You know, I don't know. I couldn't even begin to guess.

BILL: And why do you call him the Love King?

ANDREW: That's what he went by. He was called the Love King. I took a picture with him, I gave him a hug, and left wide eyed in awe. He was one of the kindest, sweetest men I have ever met in my life. One of the sweetest souls with what looked like the cosmos in his eyes. He was this big guy who roared like a lion filling me with healing love. I felt amazing all over after. At that time I was really skinny, so this guy could have flicked me and I would have fell over. He and his wife owned the store. They were both very interesting, intriguing, sweet people.

I learned later that she helps cancer patients. It's a metaphysical store that sells wigs and also statues, crystals, and other really interesting things. It was a very intriguing spot that I know I was led to by an intelligence.

The Love King showed me something that changed my life again. I didn't even tell him anything about the pain in my shoulder, he just knew about it. When he said there's stuck emotions in the body and he screamed and my arm felt much better, I began to dig deep into understanding what this all meant. Is this true that our bodies can hold onto our emotions causing us unnecessary pain? How does the body hold the emotions, store our trauma, our past experiences? How do we let these go? I began to learn all about this, how true this really is, because of this information, and it was my experience with him that showed me there's a lot more going on with our bodies than I was ever told or taught. And it led me on a very interesting path again, a very interesting journey to learn all that I could about what this meant and how emotion impacted us. How unprocessed experiences get backlogged in us causing repeated reenacted painful experiences to show up again and again. How this all is stored in our systems, our tissues, in our organs, in our bodies and how these stuck experiences in the body impact our external reality and can prevent well-being. I never saw the Love King again.

BILL: Did you do anything else while you were in Australia?

ANDREW: I didn't have much money, so my good friend Kenny and I did a lot of sightseeing. Kenny also really supported me at that time on the trip. He's an amazing friend who I consider a soul brother who has always been around during some of my biggest and toughest life experiences. He was someone who really showed up for me when father passed. I feel the main reason I was out there though was to meet the Love King. It was life changing. Right before I met Raina, I was considering, "What is my new life direction? What is it that I want to do?" And because of the therapy work, and because of the inner work I was doing on myself, I realized that I really wanted to learn all I could about human development, and potentially I was thinking about going back to school to become a therapist. I was asking reality to guide me, and what does it look like when I return from Sydney? What does this new life look like? Because it didn't feel like school was the way for me to go. That's all I knew. Like, how do I learn, how can I be of service, how can I help guide others and teach others all that I've been learning?

What began to happen was I continued to meet more and more awake healers and aligned coaches and insightful entrepreneurs, and I started looking to life coaching, and looking into becoming a coach and then began to learn everything I could learn about energy and energy medicine. I began to dig in and study and learn with open curiosity on what to do next. Eventually, I was guided to go to an amazing program at the Luminous Awareness Institute. They have two-year programs, and so far, I've done four years with them already, four years of training with them. I'm now in my 5th year. They teach a blend of work from stabilizing awake states of mind, wisdom tradition teachings, cutting edge healing and energy medicine techniques, and counseling techniques. It's a synergy of an awakening path and advanced healing arts. I use Luminous techniques blended with my own work in my current practice and life.

BILL: Where is this school based?

ANDREW: Northern California held at a retreat center they rent out in Nevada City. I felt deeply called to go there. When they came to San Diego to recruit for the two-year program, they put on an event they called a Luminous Circle where they had a gathering of people who were interested in the program. I decided to go because I was still trying to figure out what to do next.. I needed to know where to go next. I had no money. How can I afford this school? What was I going to do? I had no income. Going back to college felt like the wrong path for me.

So, I went to this event they called a Luminous Circle and about thirty people attended. They did all these interesting teachings through experiencing led by Anna-Lisa. And at this experience, they typically will pull someone in the middle of the circle that people are all standing in and they will give an example of what it's like for someone to be supported in healing using the Luminous Awareness technique. They'll work with Anna-Lisa, in the middle of the circle.

Out of all of the thirty people, she looked at me, and she asked me to come into the middle of the circle. So, I'm standing in the middle of this circle surrounded by thirty people and they created a powerful group field. She guided everyone into coherence with each other, which is like creating a really amplified field of consciousness, is the best way to describe this, of energy and consciousness in support of the well-being of whoever is in the middle. I'm in the middle of this circle and thirty people were asked to be open-heartedly holding love and care for me while I'm standing there in the middle with this powerful healer who is amazing at what she does.

She comes up to me and she points to something on the right side of my body. She's telling people that there's something blocking the flow of life energy here, there's a little bit of a block, and she then did something with her hands where she assisted the energy through my body, and at that moment I started feeling energy and vibration in my arms. I actually slowly began to shake. I had never had movement in my body like this before. It felt like two tectonic plates were being pushed together creating an earthquake inside my body. Then the energy amplified causing me to then intensely shake. You could actually see me shake. She did something else to the right side of my body, which allowed for energy to begin to freely flow, and I started to convulse.

This looked like something you would see at spiritual exorcisms, or— what are those called where you have the reverend and they do a spiritual healing? I always wondered why people would fall and they would shake and I thought that it was fake and absolutely ridiculous. Now, all of a sudden, I'm standing in the middle of thirty people shaking, and I'm feeling energy and love. I thought for a moment I was having a heart attack. I could feel my heart; it felt like it was squeezing. I looked around and thought, "Well, if I'm going to die, at least I'm dying with thirty people shining love on me. What a great way to go." I thought I was going to die because I thought I was having a stroke or a heart attack, because my left arm felt like it was numb from the vibration and the right side body was tingling from so much energy, I'm just shaking, and all this stuff is happening. Old pain was melting. Felt like life was opening me up flowing through my entire body. How could this happen from people shining open-hearted love on me? Then I felt the kind of energy that I had felt with the Love King. I felt another burst of this energy come through me in the middle of this circle and it poured through me like a waterfall of energy. It blasted out of my body again, and I was in this—the best way to describe it—this in-between space, this in-between realm of empty bliss light. I felt intense bliss and energy and deep care and infinite love and kindness. I could feel the human collective. I could feel everybody in that room. My body shook and shook and shook while bright vibrant light coursed through my entire being filling every cell.

All of a sudden, all this tension melted out of my body. I could feel places in my body I didn't know I could feel before. After she was complete, I laid on the ground for about a half hour, feeling sensations and bliss, love, and connection. Streams of wisdom flowing through me. Remembering why I came. Remembering what I was doing on this planet. After melting into the ground, I finally stood up, and without thinking I handed her a credit card and said, "I don't know what you guys are doing, but I need more of this, and I need to figure this out."

So, I gave her my card, and I affirmed, "I'm going to this program; I have to go to this school." Because that was the message I got while I was in this experience in this in-between place. I didn't know what was going on, but I thought, "I'm going to figure this out." I was told I was going to be taken care of, to be of service. This was my own choice. One of the reasons I came. So, I gave her my credit card and then throughout the years of deep trusting and fully surrendering to this flow, I was truly taken care of every month. Money came in in many interesting ways, supporting the payments for the training. I was able to pay for this school that cost, back then for me, it was about $15-20,000 total cost to go to this training with tuition, travel, food and board. I never once missed a payment. I was able to pay for everything because I was continually supported along this path. BILL: What were some of the things that you learned from this school? ANDREW: Well, a lot of the experiences that I was spontaneously experiencing prior to going to this training, I didn't have all the conceptual language for it. I was doing inner work, working on my ego, and parts work on myself that were stuck in old traumatic experiences. On my journey, I naturally began to shift into an Awake Alignment that allowed for a wise intelligence to guide me into healing my missed developmental tasks, learning personal development techniques, higher states of consciousness, and profound mystical experiences. I learned how to more deeply attune to others to guide them on their path and into their own Awake Alignment. Awake Alignment is a fully embodied, awake, always present pure aware state, with intelligent universal energy flowing through us that lives us into the world with right action that benefits the whole and guides us into deeper integration and well-being. It is beyond our everyday mind and consciousness, it is accessible to all of us, and through right action it can be stabilized in our everyday life.

I also gained more tools to work with others on their own waking up path and their growing up path, which was like the ego work I've been guided to do in my own life. How to offer healing transmissions and higher state transmissions through energy. How to heal developmental trauma that we experience and I learned more details about the safety strategies I discovered on my own path.

During the trainings, I learned a deeper understanding and language for the work I had been experiencing, how to hold my Awake Alignment, bringing in different energy qualities of consciousness and states of reality to be of benefit. I learned how to support others with cleaner attunement to their needs with these gifts and experiences I've been gifted. I learned language for the energies I was experiencing in my body. I began spontaneously feeling and seeing energies before going to this school, and I could feel people's actual belief systems, what they think and where the energy was trapped in their systems. Along with a universal wisdom that was leading and teaching me, this training helped me to deepen all those skills, gave me some detailed maps and some science for this new territory I was exploring.

All of it felt really familiar and easy for me after I met Raina. It feels like my soul already understood this work, like I've done this before in many other lives. The training was an ongoing remembrance amplifying all that I was doing. I most importantly learned that I was not the only one having these experiences on the planet. I also realized I wasn't going crazy. Because through these experiences that I'd never had before, like being in the middle of this circle, having the experience with the Love King, with Raina, part of me thought I was going a little crazy. But what I realized was that the more well that I became, the more everything around me on the planet was crazy. It felt like the world was crazy, and the saner I became, the more I realized everything was just kind of nuts.

BILL: What was the time gap between the return from the Love King and being in the circle?

ANDREW: About two and a half months.

BILL: During that two-month period, other things must have been happening that prepared you so that you would be drawn to this school.

ANDREW: Whenever I was home by myself, I would feel called into effortless meditations and I would have to just sit, and I'd begin to get visions, I'd begin to get sensations. Wisdom and spontaneous teachings about the universe would come through me. I'd feel what I now call Awake Alignment begin to arise in my system, what it feels like to be connected to my own intuition, to what I call my own essence. Energy was constantly moving through me. I would wake up almost every night with energy moving through my body, and I would be drenched in sweat and detoxing.

Old life habits would begin to drop away. After Raina, energy immediately started to move through the lower half of my stomach. Eventually, the energy cycled up through my solar plexus, through my chest, through my face. It would cycle in and out of my body, and it felt like it was cleansing me, it was detoxing me. It would incrementally clear blocks in my body and mind. I was meeting more and more people around Encinitas and in San Diego who spoke about consciousness and what people call spirituality. I continued to have experiences that were always new and fresh, and some very out-there experiences that made me begin to wonder, again, if I was going crazy.

I started seeing things all around me that were not part of my normal experience. I started seeing energies and people's faces morphing, and what looked like shape-shifting in front of me. I would see faces on them cycle from one face to another. This was a deeply confusing and interesting experience. I would know things about people, about objects they would hand me with accuracy that was impossible to be a guess. There was a point between the Love King and going to Luminous that I went and spoke with monks and then tried physicists because I was looking for an answer to see if I was going mad. Nobody had answers for me.

So, I also began to read, and I was led to online teachers like Eckhart Tolle, a lot of his books. I read Ken Wilbur's work. Energy medicine books, spiritual books, I was reading anything I felt called to; anything I got chills within my body from I kept going toward. I kept learning and experiencing. Being taught about reality from this intelligent, loving, dynamic energy that was beginning to integrate into my everyday life experience. I was having daily what people called mystical experiences with no cognitive understanding of what was happening.

One of the standout experiences was this gifted woman who people called Kamala, showed up in my life. She became an interesting teacher of mine through a coincidence, through synchronicity, a friend met this woman at a yoga studio. She was a nomadic traveler, and she said that she had come to meet his friend that he had just met that lives in inland San Diego. Kamala specifically asked to speak with Andrew—me. He called me up and said this woman is saying she has to speak with you. He said she channels this ascended master being and she needs to come talk to you. I was like, "This sounds crazy; let's do it."

So, she met me at a coffee shop on Adams Avenue in San Diego. I was quite skeptical when I first met this woman because I didn't know—what does she want, how does she know about me, why does she want to talk to me, what does this even mean? The night before I went to the coffee shop to meet her, I remember I was learning about what people call spirit guides online, and I was asking them, "Okay, if you guys really exist, prove it. I want to see you, show me, I want to know what this is." If I really have these guides that all these people are telling me about, I want to know. I demanded, "I command you to appear in front of me, I want to see you."

And they never appeared. So I thought, "Whatever, this is not real." Spirit guides? What a joke. I didn't think this was something that was real at that time. So, when I went to the coffee shop, and this woman Kamala—this is not her birth name, but this is a spiritual name she said she was given—first thing she did is she handed me a picture. She said, "This is one of your spirit guides. This is Mahavatar Babaji Maharaj and he wants me to give this to you. He's one of your teachers." I turned white. I was like, this woman, you have my attention. I don't know what you're doing or how you know this. But when she gave me this picture saying spirit guide, she now had my undivided attention. A lot of my skepticism went out the door, but I still felt a little critical just to be safe, because I didn't know what this woman wanted.

And then she told me all these things about my life that nobody would possibly know. She also knew that I was—I was wearing glasses and contacts full-time—[she knew] that I was no longer going to need these. And after seeing Raina and the Love King, my vision started to repair itself. My eyes began to heal naturally and spontaneously. I was driving one day without my glasses, and could see signs in full vibrance that I usually would struggle to see. I thought I was making that up. And she was right; a few months after meeting with her, I stopped wearing contacts and rarely used my glasses since.

BILL: Had the vision problem predated your injuries?

ANDREW: Since I was about twenty-seven, I'd needed contacts and glasses full-time. After a few months of doing this inner healing work, I rarely needed them. My vision came back spontaneously. I began to see colors and signs more clearly. Now, I only occasionally wear my glasses. Other things have spontaneously healed, a lot of problems with my stomach, painful injuries, a lot of sicknesses that I would have. I'd normally get sick throughout the year—this doesn't even happen anymore. Allergies; I no longer have seasonal allergies. Many, many things spontaneously healed the more I did this work.

And it also happens with some of my clients. A lot of my clients, they have a lot of things they begin to heal naturally and spontaneously, especially a lot of stomach problems, a lot of IBS, a lot of problems with the gut, a lot of things spontaneously just fade away. Even some old injuries get healed over time through this work. So, it's a common phenomenon.

BILL: It's not that common. I imagine a list of medical doctors who are all scratching their heads and saying, "What's going on here? How does Andrew become a healer, and what technique is he using?"

ANDREW: I use many tools in my sessions that I've learned about on this path. I continue to add new ones into my practice to support my clients with the release of stuck energy, patterns, behaviors, and addictions that are causing repeated patterns and painful experiences in everyday life. I continue working with teachers and mentors, training still to this day. I'm always a student in the world. Kamala actually became an interesting teacher of mine. She taught me for about a year. About a week after I met her, I met with her again, and she taught me techniques that she called psychic gifts.

She taught me how to read the energy of another's auric field and understand how to use this information to be of benefit. How to identify stuck energy where the natural healing wisdom was blocked and how these energy blocks caused suffering in life. She supported me in muscle testing techniques to back up my intuition with greater accuracy. She taught me how to listen more clearly to my inner wisdom to discern when its coming from ordinary conditioned mind. She explained to me that I had unique gifts to support others into their healing and how I have an ability to "activate DNA and RNA" in people during a client session. She explained how RNA was somehow connected to our past life experiences. How to assist the body's natural healing wisdom to take over to generate well-being reconnecting back to the whole. I was just staying open to what she had to share the whole time. Staying curious even though at first I was confused. At times even still wondering if this lady was a nut or maybe I was just going crazy. It eventually all became clear to me.

During our second meeting before we began any trainings, something so amazing happened that really put my inner critic to rest. In my calendar that month, I had written "deposit check." I needed to put money into my account. Had to find a way to pay so that was my reminder because I was all out of money. I still had no income and I didn't know how I was going to pay all my bills and my rent. There was a specific amount I needed at that time to cover it all. I was doing all this work to try to create abundance because everyone talks about manifestation, they're telling me that I need to manifest and create. I was doing the best that I could to try to figure out how to make money at that time. I knew I could go get a regular job if I had to to but I couldn't bring myself to go back into that world. It never felt right. I just had to stay on this new path.

A lot of these things that I was hearing at that time about visioning, they weren't really working yet, so I just kept my practice going on, not giving into fear, surrendering and meditating. Deeply opening myself to the guidance of the universe. Holding my intention to get out of this debt. I remember putting on my calendar "deposit check" to remind me to go out and take action to make some money. The due dates were coming up fast, and fear was beginning to deepen. I again felt this inner call to just surrender and meditate with kindness into this fear. My inner critic was going crazy and wanted me to go out and do something to make money. I knew I couldn't give into this money fear, that no matter what happened, I would survive.

When I met up with Kamala, a week after I met her for the first time, we met at a café right down the street from your place here in Cardiff. I was sitting with her, and again just like she did the first time I met her, she surprised me. Out of nowhere the first thing she did when I sat down was slide me a check without saying a word. Well actually, she did say, "Your guide Mahavatar Babaji Maharaj wants me to give this to you." I looked at the check. It was the exact amount I needed to pay my bills. I sat there, in front of this woman, holding this check up and just cried.

Tears of deep joy and sadness pouring out of me at this café. Nobody knew that I needed this money, nobody had any idea that I needed to deposit money into my account the next day. Not a friend, nobody. Just me. I just cried in this café. I felt so held, so supported, something I had never felt before in my life. Kamala said this Being she is channeling is telling her to give me money. No strings attached. It was just unbelievable. How could this be happening?

Kamala supported me in many ways when she was in my life. She gave me money, taught me how to give aligned healing sessions, she explained the value of my gifts, explained how to charge my worth, and trained me in many techniques to use with clients. I did many sessions with her and she would pay me a substantial amount to do sessions on her. She would always say Mahavatar Babaji Maharaj before any sentence she spoke, that's how she would say it every time, "Mahavatar Babaji Maharaj needs you to do a session on me, he wants to teach you something," or, "Do a session on this person, I'm going to pay you for them." She paid me. She gave me money for a year straight to support me. She would pay for others to receive sessions from me as well.

Eventually, we went on a silent retreat to Mt. Shasta with twelve people; six she paid for to fly in from Switzerland and six from the U.S. It was this amazing retreat, we all did a lot of powerful healing work on Mt. Shasta led by Kamala who was being instructed by the ascended master Babaji. I had no clue how I ended up here, but it was amazing. I could feel and see so much going on that I never thought was possible before. She taught me all these amazing insights again and again. And after this silent retreat she said, "Mahavatar Babaji Maharaj says I have to leave, I'm going away on a new journey and I most likely will never see you again." And she left. This amazing woman never asked me for anything in return. Ever.

BILL: Kamala seems like a much more powerful experience than the Love King. The Love King was another catalyst, but it seems to me that Kamala was really your true guardian angel.

ANDREW: One of the many. She was one really important guardian angel. The Love King was exactly what I needed and could handle at that time. When Kamala arrived, I was available for her experience by then. I had to be ready because I wouldn't have been able to trust this kind of support in the past.

BILL: One of the things that I'm seeing is you are not a model for what other people can do, because I don't think planning on a guardian angel showing up and taking care of you is most people's workout regimen.

ANDREW: Understood. You know, Bill, when I first started this work, like I said, I wasn't looking for any of this, right? I got into this work to feel better. I didn't know any of this was going to happen. All this started spontaneously. The one thing that stands out through all this experience is that the control of my conditioning, this inner voice is no longer running the show, telling me not to go be with any of these people, like the Love King, Kamala. If that voice was still telling me what to do—because it told me not to listen to Kamala; it was like, "You're getting into some sort of cult with this woman, what are you doing." It told me to get out of the Love King's house. If I hadn't surrendered into what felt right, truly felt right, none of this would have happened. Discernment is an important tool to sharpen and to have in the world, but we can't let our fear win over our true intuition.

BILL: So, you had an inner dialogue of the old Andrew telling you to flee, and the new inner witness telling you to stay.

ANDREW: It was a deeper inner voice coming from my being, from my heart, telling me to stay. Not my mind or inner critic. Kamala impacted many people around me. A friend I was with at the time also received a check, the exact amount she needed as well. Kamala did so much for so many without question. She was an intriguing person. She followed her truth no matter how odd or unconventional it was. Most people thought she was crazy because she was saying "Mahavatar Babaji Maharaj" before every sentence.

She handed me a picture of him, one of my spirit teachers, in that first meeting. Babaji is the person that brought Kriya yoga to the world and created the lineage of the Self Realization Fellowship that Yogananda established here in Encinitas. He's what they call an avatar. He was a teacher of Yogananda and the original teacher who brought Kriya Yoga to the world. Yogananda was a student of Sri Yukteswar, and he was a student of somebody else who Babaji manifested into reality and taught. Some say he was never actually born into a human body. He apparently showed up out of nowhere and gave this spiritual technology to help people fully realize Spirit.

BILL: And so, of the things that you were taught, can you now teach what you were taught? Can you teach others how to read auras, how to see etheric beings?

ANDREW: I do. I teach some clients specific techniques that work with their own tools and their own gifts that I was taught through Kamala and some other teachers. I use a blend of what all my teachers have taught me and a lot of what I learned from my own meditation, my own experiences. Reality has taught me something that I was trained in. Some clients ask how to do certain things like track energy, see energies, I do teach that as well. Anybody can learn this.

What I believe and experienced is that people have certain information in their essence, who maybe had other experiences in other lives, who have these cultivated skill-sets that are part of their soul blueprint waiting to be activated. We can unlock our greatest gifts with the right guidance. Some people are more sensitive to energies or others have greater access to present dimensions that may have wisdom to share with us. Some may have other gifts that a person who is highly sensitive might not have. There are many different types of gifts and technologies in our bodies and souls that we have access to. Everybody has access to their own unique gifts that are waiting to be unlocked.

BILL: It seems to me that the most important quality would be desire. You have to have the desire to learn. For instance, I personally am not interested. I don't care what your aura is. I don't want to track your energy. I'm tracking my own and I'm fine.

ANDREW: I try to use my gifts in alignment with my life commitments. We don't ever want to get fixated on gifts but I believe that they can be used for benefit when acting from spiritual maturity. One of the things I am committed to is being of service through the deepening my own inner work. Also committed to my own awakening path, guiding others that are open, and to have a unique exciting adventure of a life. I don't ever want to waste this blessing of human life that I have been gifted. I currently use my gifts to do that in the world.

BILL: I think it's important to make that point, because as we develop the skills that you're going to teach in the rest of this book, I think it is a Chinese menu: you don't have to eat everything.

ANDREW: That's right. It'd be too much.

BILL: If there's a specific skill you are seeking, great. And if there are skills here that don't interest you, that's perfectly fine.

ANDREW: Absolutely. What I also learned through my own experiences is that even prior to any of these experiences, that most of my life I've been highly sensitive to energies, even before I did any of this work. As I look back, this is something I've always had. I just didn't consciously realize it. I didn't consciously know how to use them. Now, I can consciously use my gifts in my work and to be of benefit.

BILL: The other thing that I've observed is that you are highly motivated now, because you were searching for a purpose, and when you identified this as your purpose, that opened the floodgates for you to learn and for people like magical Kamala to show up, and enhance your gifts.

ANDREW: Yes. It created an epic adventure that I could not have predicted. Not only do I have this sense of inner purpose to be of service and to share what I've learned, not only for me and others, but it's been fun. We are not taught about stuck emotion, we are not taught about soul's greatest gifts. It's up to us to break free of our social norms if we want to experience all that reality has to offer us. Commitment is a key ingredient to that. It's has to be our choice. On this journey we must become so comfortable with being uncomfortable. You have to go against society's rules, and that can, at times, be tough without a high level of commitment to something greater fueling the journey. Through our intention we have the power to consciously choose what we wish to learn through in life. All we have to do is choose. I choose love.

CHAPTER SIX
LIVING IN TWO WORLDS

BILL: As we've observed in the previous description of experiences that Andrew had, first with the Love King, and then with Kamala, and with Luminous, all these experiences are creating a new reality for him. Andrew, you seem to be living in two worlds. How did you evolve so you could integrate the old Andrew with the new Andrew?

ANDREW: Living in two worlds is the perfect description of what it's been like throughout this unfolding. At times, my reality does feel split between old habits of self and new ways of being. As I was experiencing these new experiences and sharing them with people I care about, they didn't understand what was happening to me, so there was a part of me that felt isolated. At times, I felt very isolated.

Then there's this other side of me that's having these amazing experiences, felt very connected, very held and supported, and I was really enjoying this reality. Confusion of what exactly was going on would continue to challenge my new reality. Why are these experiences happening to me, or through me, or what is really going on? So, with that split, I was living in two worlds. I had old friends who didn't understand me anymore. I continued to evolve and continued to grow, because there was nothing I could do about it; life was beginning to live through me.

There was a momentum about it and I really wanted to see where this was going to end up. Everywhere I went, I was being led and continued to surrender. I felt that commitment was within my essence; it was my essence moving me one way, and these old ego structures that were scared trying to slow me down. As I evolve, I eventually could see there was a lag time for the reality to fully stabilize and for old habits to die out and old parts to fully catch up. With compassion and love for all the old habits and parts, eventually the new reality would become the normal reality, and this would then happen again. It was a cycle of transformation, letting go, processing, integration and stabilization of the new in its own timing. BILL: Did you have to curtail your ego structures when you were doing your new things? Or did you have to curtail your new reality when you were associating with your old world, or both?

ANDREW: It became where it just was what it was. Whatever was happening, no matter where it was happening, I had to allow it. I had to bring in discernment with my behaviors, and acceptance was key to accelerating the new way of being. Friends in my old world couldn't understand the new world. As hard as that was at times I had to be okay with that, to accept that reality. This new world was evolving on its own into something new. The old structures started to create a whole new persona.

At one time on my path, spiritual ego began to form. I noticed it because I had these energetic gifts that were rapidly coming online in my life, these psychic abilities, and there was even a point that I thought I was some sort of savior. I must be some savior healer, here to do all this work and save people in the world. It was a strange confused feeling that started to show up in me. I finally realized, "Oh, the ego's looking for a place to land." It's looking for a safe place to explain what's happening in my life. To find a new identity to grab onto. It was far off the mark. I quickly let that idea go and deeply know that I am not a savior or here to save anyone. I can support others into their own natural wisdom and power that exists in us all.

I realized I had all these amazing abilities, but also, how do I navigate reality and still be human and still explore these amazing aspects of reality? I've realized that people on this path can typically either go into spirit or pure emptiness, essentially bypassing ego or human, or they get stuck in human ego and lost in the body and small everyday mind only, ignoring Spirit. What I began to realize is that you can have both by integrating into an Awake Alignment operating in well-being. Human, soul and Spirit are interconnected, not separate. Different parts of a complex system just like the whole of you and I. A part of the whole and the whole all in one, interconnection through all inter-being. Never actually separate. Always connected to the universe. We can integrate these parts into everyday life and live them into the world.

If you can learn to allow the wisdom of pure awareness in the universe to guide you, it will show you how to integrate the ego, soul and pure essence, and you can live from your spark or pure essence and still have a personality without all the identities and attachments, without all the unnecessary fear, without all the unnecessary pain, and still be in the world transcending unnecessary suffering. Actually, you will have an even greater impact in the world. There is a power in this integration that flows through everything. We can access the very power of creation, that power that created all things. Such a wonderful gift.

BILL: This is one of the reasons I wanted you to do this chapter, because I think it's very important for people who are in transition, because for many people, you don't have to become a healer to start using some of these skills and abilities, and to become more aware. I think one of the challenges is going off the deep end and losing your quote, "identity," and losing your family and friends. If you could speak a little bit about how you were able to maintain, and maybe you weren't, because in some cases, some people you are going to lose. I would imagine that for people who knew the old Andrew, some of these new skills and activities must have seemed very strange.

ANDREW: That's right. Most people would say to me, "Well, if you're happy, I'm happy for you." Because they didn't know how to digest or understand my experiences. There were times where I did go off the deep end. I lost my entire personality and was just merged into a pure state of everything. There was always a knowing inside that I was on the right path. After my experience with Raina, this was always clear. All the fear that was in there had dissipated and I wasn't operating from a place of fear, but my human side felt alone and isolated. I felt I couldn't connect with anybody anymore.

At that time, it was strange because all these amazing experiences happened, but a part of me felt lonely and isolated. And there was a part that still felt very scared. Will I be able to actually be human again? Is there room for both these realities? As months went on, and time went on, I was taught from a pure intelligent awareness how to integrate myself back, learned how to ground back into my body, back into reality, and work through some fear-based old personality behaviors, and lovingly dissolve old parts that were still existing and operating inside me. I began to navigate and interact with reality from my personality vehicle without being lost in it as opposed to this unattuned, disassociated, un-integrated person with no personality who's screaming about love being everywhere that everyone must feel.

BILL: Well, the enlightenment experience, if you can't share it, what's the point of it?

ANDREW: That was one of the first thoughts that came through my personality after I had my experience with Raina, is how do I tell everybody about what's really in front of us? I care so deeply and I really wanted to share with everyone, and I needed to find a way to share. You have to be ready for it, or I guess at least get yourself ready to be available for that grace. It's a grace that no person can give to another. Most people just thought I was insane.

BILL: But what you learn, of course, is that it's not your experience to share. It's how do you integrate the experience of those who you are with toward enlightenment for them? Because otherwise you're creating separation rather than integration.

ANDREW: What I've realized is that it's not my place to convince anyone of anything. One of the biggest realizations I've had, I'm here to be me fully. Authentically me and that shift in me will create shifts outside of me. That means I need to fully let go of a lot of old habits of self that I have been using all my life. And if someone wants guidance, or my path and my experiences inspire, I'm happy to offer it. To have a real impact, the more I deepen my own work, embody it in the world, the greater impact I can have. That's how I can be of support. Focus on my own depth and deepen my own realizations to live them into the world. I'm deeply committed to my inner path and to pick up as many tools and gifts to use along that way to be of service the best that I can.

BILL: Well, what we can all give, including you, in whatever state you're in, and the reader in whatever state they may be in, is when you give focused attention to another and are able to have empathy and sensitivity toward where they are insofar as you show up for them, you enable them to continue on their journey. Obviously, you need to be selective because certain people are vibrating at such a level that you can't connect at all anymore.

ANDREW: There must be a willingness. An openness to face parts of us we don't want to face. To face a reality we ignore or are afraid to look at.

BILL: It's not so much there must be a willingness, but you are still you, and you have an obligation to your own journey not to get off your path. If you walked into a den of people who were all shooting up heroin, you don't say, "Oh, this is fine for you." You walk away. However, there are those with little dust, those who are at the point of awakening, and those people just by meeting them where they are, you can have a great positive impact upon them.

ANDREW: One of the most important things I learned on this path that I feel is worth mentioning again is that through me doing more of my own inner work, the greater impact I can have, through me continuing what I do with myself is what really matters. This is my focus; this is my current commitment. To fully embody the wisdom, realizations and love into the world, knowing that everyone I work with has their own natural wisdom and intelligence. Sometimes it just needs a jumpstart.

BILL: And part of it is, as you say, you're not really doing anything, you're just showing up fully present.

ANDREW: That's it, yes. With deep care and love, with a focused intention on their essential wellness. Letting go of expectation resting into my Awake Alignment best that I can. Whoever's in front of me, there's that true intention to be fully there, to be of service, knowing that they all are fully capable of reaching their unlimited potential. Because there's a real care I have for all who stand in front of me. Including myself. I have to include myself in the whole because if I didn't include me in all that I do, I am now creating separation as well. Wholeness includes the self.

There are many out there supporting others from an under-resourced place because they forgot to include themselves in the work. I once lived this way. I couldn't have the impact I now have without including the self. Sometimes we don't know how to do that, so figuring that out may be the first thing to do. My inward turn was me beginning to include myself in my own life. With love, with care.

BILL: Knowledge is a very simple, basic human kindness. We're taught this in almost every major religion, and if you have a nice mother and father, they teach this to you—be kind to others. And it works. And life can be that simple. It's just the actual expression of this is not as easy as we would like it to be.

ANDREW: What I currently notice to be true is the more I release my identification to these old ego structures and integrate them with love and embrace all that I am, the deeper the care that arises out of an Awake Alignment for others. It's a natural compassion and care that is within all of us. The more we integrate our own parts, our own structures, it's there. Love is there, care is there. Love is the very fabric of our being.

BILL: That's why, in terms of integration of a more aware, more spiritually oriented being, in a normal, everyday guy, gal, father, mother, child, it's in these very basic practices that you achieve integration.

ANDREW: Through the years of this work, I developed my maps and life navigation tools that helped guide me. They supported me to reorient back into my pure Awake Alignment when I was off. Life maps and a life compass that I used in my everyday life to keep me on my path, purpose, and commitments. Many of these maps developed out of the territory of exploration of my own integration work, healing work, all the different spiritual paths that exist, all the different wisdom traditions. I started to realize that a lot of these things pointed to the same thing. I naturally developed my own maps to fit my own unique path that I use within my own work and with my clients. I still continue to use and refine these life tools within myself, and that's one of the things that came out of the ongoing integration work. I was deep in the territory. I could see that these maps can easily be given to others through experiences in my sessions for others, and to offer point-outs, a direction, where to go and what to do to guide others into their own authentic Awake Alignment and natural wisdom. An attuned set of life tools and experiences can help us accelerate this work greatly.

BILL: One of the expressions you use is that you discovered a new operating system that was heart-mind based.

ANDREW: For me, the way I look at it is, from a larger perspective on this planet, we are shifting. Something I've realized within my own work, and I have heard others speak of this very thing, that confirmed what I realized through my own meditation work, my own inner healing work, is that we're all going through a major shift at this time. You mentioned this earlier, I think it was chapter three or four, where the planet is shifting, and humanity is rapidly evolving. We're moving away from this idea of achievements, getting out of this lost state, this sleeping state of mind. A massive awakening is taking place. Whether we are conscious of it or not, it is occurring. Has been occurring. Has already occurred and we are just stepping into what has always been. Achievements are beautiful, and achieving is a skill set we should keep, and we should continue to have that, but no longer identify with it. Care for each other and this planet is of far greater value. Be of service to benefit the whole.

We're moving into a higher, already present, more intelligent operating system that includes our hearts, our minds, and our full system into an Awake Alignment. As we integrate all the way through our system, our hearts open, there's a new way we can make heart-based intelligent decisions that include the whole—not only from logic, or just from what we think we want, or desire based on conditioning. We now have conscious choice to take right action from real care and compassion, and to think of the whole based on how our actions are going to impact the whole entire planet; not only the planet, but the cosmos, because we are so interconnected that every action ripples through everything, everywhere. All time, All space, All beings. We're moving into a time-space where we take aligned awake action from our heart and bring a blend of balance between the heart and the mind.

It's already there in us, but it needs to be turned on by getting out of the way. This type of inner work begins to naturally move us into it. You can't force heart-mind; it's effortless, and it begins to rise through this work, through deepening our care and compassion for ourselves so we can deepen our care and compassion for others. Heart-mind or an Awake Alignment is an operating system that is naturally rising in the collective through the individuals who are doing this work. We're not doing it by ourselves. We can't; it can't be done by ourselves; we have to do it all together. Deep down, the commitment to what I do is to be of service to guide others into that very thing so they can live their fullest life and live in love and care, as their actions ripple through the cosmos.

BILL: This is the side of everything matters. We've talked about when you're in the enlightenment state, nothing matters and everything matters. And the "nothing matters" is from the perspective of the all-that-is, the energy that is the source of all source; nothing really matters because energy is eternal and perfect. From the point of view of human beings and all of life, and even inanimate objects, "everything matters" because once you leave the sacred space of no space, you are subject to cause and effect and all of the laws of physics and everything else that we use to have life experiences.

At that level, absolutely everything matters because everything is interconnected. I think what you're talking about in the new operating system is the awareness that this is true. It's not just words. And it's true, not just intellectually, but it's true emotionally and it's true at the level of the heart. One of the things we're discovering is the true meaning of the heart. The word and metaphor of the heart has been used throughout human existence. Broken heart, heartthrob. We use the concept of heart in so many different ways.

We need to return to a new understanding of what heart-centered really means. One of the clients that we've had the pleasure of representing for many years is HeartMath. HeartMath is one of the institutions that has played the largest role in bringing this new awareness of the importance of integrating the intellect with the heart, and realizing, and this is actually scientifically validated, that the organ within the body that generates the most energy is not the brain, but the heart. So when we say the heart of the matter, we are really talking about the heart.

ANDREW: Absolutely.

BILL: What pointers do you have, and it's interesting you use the concepts of maps—Eckhart uses pointers, he's always saying pointers. What are some of the pointers and techniques that you developed, that not only have been useful for you in creating this integration, but useful for your clients?

ANDREW: We are part of a larger system. The part of the whole that we are is actually its own complex system with many levels, many lines of development, and we are on a journey through stages and cycles. Sometimes things get missed or skipped over on our developmental journey, causing us to have a sense deep within that something is missing. This unknown experience in a stage of development can cause us a lot of unnecessary suffering in our life. With proper maps, we are able to navigate or locate where we currently are on our journey or what we may have missed to go back to repair those missed experiences, maybe even redo some of the developmental stages and experiences we missed as a child.

This, at times, quickly helps fix many areas of our lives and releases many addictions, problems that keep occurring. Good life maps are amazing tools, can help us find our way in reality, they can guide us and help us adjust back on course and get out of suffering loops. Typologies are a type of map I enjoy using that help us understand our own unique systems, ways of behaving and operating in the world.

Personality Character Structures are another type of map that can support us with identifying our defensive safety strategies we use and have been using to keep us alive and safe since childhood. Another powerful map is learning some basics about attachment theory and our go-to attachment style while in connection. Repairing the human attachment system using attachment therapies is another way to support us into deeper well-being and makes it easier to shift into our Awake Alignment. One important thing to note is maps are wonderful, but they are absolutely not the territory. It's like looking at a GPS map can give you an idea of where to go to find a city, but when you arrive at the city, at the territory, there is so much to enjoy—beauty, food, wonder, people, experiences, art and more that the map could never offer. Maps eventually have to be dropped. We have to put them down, put the books down, put the ideas down and be with the direct experience of the territory. Use maps to point us to healing, to integrate our system and eventually live from our Awake Alignment using our greatest gifts with right action in the world. We can create detailed maps of our entire system that can be of benefit as long as we don't get fixated and attached to those maps. Reality is always changing. Maps become outdated.

We are not the maps, the ideas, the thoughts we may use to navigate. Many get lost in the maps or use too many maps. When used properly, mapping out parts of our system like energetics, our behaviors, our safety strategies can be of great use to help us evolve and to go back to fill in missed experiences that may still be causing us problems today in our energy systems, nervous systems, everyday lives, health, and relationships and a whole lot more.

That's what I began to do at the beginning of this journey, I began to develop my own maps through reflective awareness, which was me becoming a mirror for myself by staying in this mode of curious open observation, and sitting and watching what's really happening no matter what was arising in me. My system began to map itself. Then pointed me into the proper direction for healing and integration. Cultivating reflective awareness was absolutely key to this work. There are so many maps we can read or find in the world, but I find our own reflective awareness, which leads to self-awareness, is a foundational aspect of any type of inner work.

If we're not aware of what's happening, and we assume we think we know what's going on, then we can get really lost. We can pick a map, or a life compass—the light of pure Awake Awareness is like the compass. Do I go left here, or do I go right here? If you go left when you're supposed to go right down a street, you're going to have a very different destination. You need to know where you're going. Having reflective awareness is really why you're doing what you're doing. It's important to see where you're going, so you don't continue to crash and end up in the same repeated painful experiences, not knowing why, over and over again.

I like to find ways to support clients to cultivate this skill in their own system and to live it in their everyday lives. One beautiful technique I use is effortless open breath awareness to strengthen the ability to rest in a pure open restful state to stay in the territory you are investigating. Breath is always there to become aware of from our open pure awareness that all form is rising and falling in. If you watch your breath with easeful open awareness, what begins to happen is you develop a muscle of becoming more present with whatever is arising in your field of experience. It also has a positive impact on the well-being of the body. It seems to lower stress, lowers cortisol, heart rate balances. There's a lot of positive aspects to watching breath. If you continue to watch your breath from effortless open awareness, you grow that muscle to be able to observe what's really happening without getting merged into the experience. You can observe your mind; you begin to see your own thought forms that constantly rise and fall in effortless pure awareness. As you develop more of this skill, you start to pull the plug on the power of the mind, and then you begin to watch it, the mind seems to slow down, time disappears, tension melts away, joy begins to bubble up more and more and the mind gap widens between thought forms.

It's very simple; your breath is always there. Become aware of your breath from an open relaxed awareness without effort, without trying to change it. This is a very powerful technique, and it's very simple. Anybody can do it. I do it while driving. I just notice my breath from my awareness and if I forget, I just come back without judgment, and just return to the breath. Observing the breath is one of the techniques that, whoever's doing work with me, I always tell them to watch their breath from open awareness, which is different than a focused concentrated mind attention. Attention can not be maintained, an open awareness can stay effortlessly focused and lovingly hold anything. Breath is one of many doorways to this open effortless pure awareness. There's many other skill-sets and techniques that build upon this. Everyone can power up their own awareness and learn to liberate their small self consciousness, while resting as the pure state of awareness. This builds our ability to focus fully into the Now without being swept away by thoughts into the past and future. This is one of many simple techniques that is extremely powerful when it's done every day with dedication. I've used it for many years now and it has guided me into a more stabilized life of well-being.

BILL: The less you try, the more you achieve, because you're no longer trying to achieve.

ANDREW: Absolutely. Life navigation tools, like reflective awareness, allow for more ease and flow in life. We can point our ship, align our system, and let flow take you to the next amazing destination to explore. No need to try so hard. Life is an awake flow. To me, everything in life can be used as a map or a mirror pointing the way back home, back to Self and back into Awake Alignment.

CHAPTER SEVEN
LETTING GO OF EXPECTATION

BILL: We were going to start this chapter about how letting go is one of the keys to create integration, and how, as you increase your awareness, you are living, so to speak, in two worlds at once—the world you were programmed to live in, and then the world that actually exists that you're just becoming aware of.

One of the very interesting things that happened during the creation of this book is that Andrew has just had an event today in which energies that he was not anticipating have forced him to confront, on a higher level, the need to integrate these energies with his present state, even though it's much more integrated than it was several years ago when he was first confronting this new awareness. Andrew, tell the readers a little bit about what you're experiencing right now in terms of the lack of integration that you're feeling in this moment.

ANDREW: I feel ungrounded, a bit off my center, and I'm not feeling like my everyday self, the alignment that normally feels centered and grounded during these healing and book writing sessions. I feel unfocused and there's a little bit of fear and anxiety that is present. There is a part of me that wants to run away from all of this unease, run away from the experience and not feel any of this discomfort.

BILL: When you say "run away from the experience," you're talking about running away from the energies that are going through you?

ANDREW: Yes, the anxiety that's inside me. A part of me does not want to feel the fear that's in me or the anxiety that's in me at this very moment. A part of me wants to run out of here and not write. Doesn't want to bring an anxious transmission into this book writing. Doesn't want to "look bad" or risk being judged for not writing something insightful. Another part of me is excited for what's about to happen as we have decided to move forward and write from this authentic experience of unease. All of these experiences and more are rising and falling within me.

BILL: Explain where this fear is, what experience you just had, what energy you experienced earlier today. And it may be a little out there for some readers, but it's your experience, so let's just dig in.

ANDREW: Every day I orient to my true, authentic Awake Alignment using my practices and many life navigation tools I gained along my path. I have my morning routine and things that I do to stay centered to approach my day. Throughout this journey I have had what some call mystical experiences and meditations that get pretty wild, where powerful energy moves through my body. At times, I have the experience of information coming through me from many places, which I feel to be from out in the cosmos and from deep within me. I have experienced ecstatic bliss to detailed visions, as well as experiences of beautiful visual gold light that pours through all the objects in the room and rings out with love. Sometimes these spontaneous experiences are wonderful and at other times I have experiences that are a lot for me to hold.

Today, with my beautiful girlfriend Felicia, we did a weekly practice where we session each other with a connection exercise to deepen our connection to each other. We use this amazing healing tool called the Adult Attachment Repair Model from a talented psychotherapist, Peter Cummings. This practice was developed out of his life's work. For over forty years, he's been in practice helping people heal from attachment trauma and developmental trauma.

He developed this amazing tool to rewire the human attachment system. It has forever changed my life, rewiring my system to operate from the optimal social engagement system, supporting me into even greater well-being. His powerful tool has helped both Felicia and I deepen our intimacy, connect from an embodied heart based connection, and has supported us both to learn to meet each other's needs.

Understanding the human attachment system is really important to healing and processing trauma, bonding, connection, opening to others, well-being, reducing anxiety and this list goes on. I feel that it's so important for us all to understand the attachment system to deepen our baseline of well-being. Developmental attachment trauma, in my opinion, is currently causing much of the isolation and loneliness we are all facing today. Just look around and we can see in our country how hard it is for people to fully connect and stay connected. I'm not just speaking to staying together as separate islands in a relationship. But truly staying open and lovingly connected while staying together. This authentic connection generates greater well-being and health in our life. From my experience, anyone that has trouble in relationships and connecting with others would benefit greatly from understanding and rewiring their attachment system, which also directly connects to the optimal functioning of the vagus nerve. This system he created to heal the human attachment system has profoundly changed many lives for the better, including my own. Peter, as well as my clients and others who use this tool, refer to it as stick work.

Today, we were using a modified version of Peter's modality to connect, where I first supported her. We then switch sides. After I supported Felicia through her session, she felt resourced, relaxed and connected. My experience was the opposite of hers.

BILL: In Peter's method, there's a stick that both individuals hold and is used to convey, at least symbolically and energetically, the sharing of energy, creating a circuit of connection, allowing for the processing of experiences to occur.

ANDREW: It does create a circuit and a connection that most people can feel during the process. Using Peter's method, my entire life has shifted for the better and a deep felt sense of embodied safety has now been integrated throughout my entire system by incrementally rewiring my attachment system over the last few years. Peter is an attachment system genius who I've been really lucky to learn and heal from for the past four years. One person holds aligned space, the practitioner, as a resource, as a safe, secure base, a grounded presence, and then on the other side, the person will feel that connection, feel supported, and will eventually be able to integrate and naturally move through past experiences or information that's stuck in their system or energies or emotions that need to be integrated.

It guides the receiver into the natural healing wisdom of the body; the intelligence of our universe does the work. I, personally, can feel that Peter has created an integrative method that balances, heals, and naturally rewires our entire system, allowing for our human parts, soul parts, and spiritual parts to flow in coherence through our entire body and nervous system. It is the optimal way that our system wants to flow.

When Felicia was holding space and presence for me today, things were moving as usual and I started feeling a deeper sense of well-being in my system. Energy was processing, backlogged emotions that were bogging me down were easefully moving through. I felt grounded and safe and things were amazing. All of a sudden, Felicia and I both started having this highly intense, spontaneous energetic experience. For a few minutes, we didn't really share the experience out loud, but eventually Felicia started talking about some visions she was seeing. And she was seeing pyramids, she was seeing Egypt, and I, surprisingly, was seeing the exact same thing.

I started seeing a 360-degree view of Egypt, and I was seeing above the pyramid and Felicia was having the same detailed visuals. She was receiving all kinds of information. And then I stopped sharing and she was naming exactly what I was seeing and what was happening inside of me. We were having this spontaneous experience together and suddenly this loud voice started to rise up in the background of my mind and it was "I am Ra," is what it was saying. I know there's a deity "Ra." I've heard of a deity Ra. I don't follow or know much about this deity or worship the deity Ra in any way, but this is something that was coming through me. Blasting through my body with a huge charge of ungrounding energy that I could not generate myself.

Felicia, even before I told her this experience was happening to me, mentioned that she could feel this or hear this voice saying that "I am Ra." So as this big energy is moving through me, it feels like the internal wattage is being amplified, the wattage is being amplified through my body, and it's starting to create unease in the body. Eventually, as I'm connected with

Felicia, that energy, that unease, actually started feeling good. It started feeling like well-being at first. As energy is pouring through me, I could feel some processing of past experiences happening. I could tell it was not looping, it was resolving, so I'm trying not to interrupt the experience. I'm deciding to stay aligned and allowing this experience to move through me, surrendering into it. The more I surrender, the better it is feeling.

However, as we're continuing through this process, I noticed there was almost too much energy starting to run through me, and I noticed myself splitting in a way where I was becoming unembodied and, again, ungrounded. I felt disoriented. Felicia was naming what she was going through with these experiences. She was having accurately profound interpretations and visuals of what the experience looked like visually. I was seeing them as well, so we were confirming them with each other.

Interestingly enough, we rarely see cats around my place, but a cat showed up right in front of my door at this time and looked through the glass window of the door. In that very same moment before the cat appeared, we're both seeing internal imagery of cats as well.

BILL: Well, just to make a point, in Egypt, cats were worshiped.

ANDREW: I didn't know that until after this session, because I wanted to look up the meaning of cats. I felt like it would be interesting to look into that. Felicia also had the thought that maybe I should look up what cat totems were, and we started looking, and there was a whole connection with Egypt and cats. The point of us using a modified versions of Peter's stick work was to deepen in connection on a human level, and this interesting, wild energetic ride showed up out of nowhere.

Felicia and I found a way to use his method to safely connect deeper with each other. For her, she had her own normal experiences and it was a straightforward session for her. But for me, I'm just looking to deepen embodied alignment and relax into well-being to go about my human day and enjoy, and rest into my Awake Alignment, to then come here feeling grounded and ready to continue to explore writing this book. I have this idea of how I'm going to show up at your place being in alignment, relaxed and ready to hopefully bring some amazing content through for this chapter. A part of me has this expectation to be at my fullest. To show up in a way to flow and sound great for the readers. And I show up here, and as time gets closer, I'm still feeling anxious, disoriented. Putting pressure on myself to get it right, to perform. I show up right here now with you, Bill, and I'm trying to write this book, and I feel anxious, disoriented and confused. Derailed from some unexpected energy from Egypt.

BILL: Well, this is good because the chapters about earlier in your life, when you just start to have these experiences after Raina and Kamala and the Love King, you were dealing with similar anxieties related to your new awareness and your old programming. So in a sense, this is the same gestalt, but perhaps intensified and slightly stranger, because first, it's a shared experience, it involves a deity, at least for many people, a deity. So I think we need to bring it back to everyday reality.

First of all, you're not saying, "Oh, the voice of Ra through me," you're not thinking you're Ra, you're just experiencing, and you're aware that what you're experiencing is not a fantasy; it's based on something that's real. Now you're in a situation where this energy is a lot stronger than my everyday reality energy, and how do I integrate that experience with my everyday reality? I mean, I'm supposed to be here writing a book. I don't know, maybe you had a client today; hopefully not. But this is one of the challenges for people who are going to be reading and listening to this book because the goal is not to enter a level of awareness that destroys your everyday reality; it's to integrate the new awareness with your everyday reality, and to hopefully enhance your everyday reality.

So, this is what you're struggling with today. Let's see if we can create some integration right here, right now, which can also serve as a model for people who are going through similar, though hopefully less intense, out of body experiences.

ANDREW: I find it interesting that this happened today during this chapter, that again to me doesn't feel like a coincidence. Reality, for me, in the past I'd hold it to a certain expectation. I did come here with an expectation. I have to lovingly laugh at my own expectations. I go into my client sessions with an expectation of how I need to show up. And every single time, without fail since I've experienced that wonderful explosion with Raina, I have learned that I just have to always lovingly let go of my expectations. I have to surrender to what is. In the past, if I was writing this book with you, after I had that experience, I would have run out of here and cancelled this writing session to come back next week and try to be perfect.

BILL: This is interesting, because where we left off at the previous chapter was that one of the best techniques for integration is letting go, letting go of expectations, and letting go of the discomfort that you may feel in having two worlds that aren't necessarily in sync.

ANDREW: Yes. Resting in an expanded awareness, accepting the current situation as it is, we are making the best of it. As we're talking about it, there's a sense of a more groundedness starting to show up inside me. There's a part of me that still has an expectation of how I want this to be perfect, how I want to be amazing at what I share, and there's also a part of me that's afraid of what people might think when I talk about this "I am Ra" that's going through me. This is not something that I ever feel like I wanted to share. In the past, I would have considered someone to be crazy talking about this kind of stuff. Now here I am, openly sharing this wild experience.

BILL: Well, I had hesitation just before we started the chapter. I said no, no. This book doesn't include Ra. Ra is a little out there. Save Ra for a second book. But as we learned, well, we couldn't really do that. Because you can't get away from Ra right now. It's a good example of how you can't force things. If you as a reader are, right now, having an experience of dissonance between your programmed reality and the reality you're stepping into, don't run away from it, because you can't.

ANDREW: That's right. Within this dynamic that we're currently in right now, sitting here, I feel supported. I'm not alone with my experience. So, I'm also able to receive support from you which is helping the integration of this.

BILL: One of the other things that's important in terms of the general reader is, throughout your own journey, you've had moments when other people thought you were crazy, and then moments when you thought you might be crazy.

ANDREW: Very true. It's felt isolating that people thought I was crazy or weird. I never looked for these spontaneous experiences. They just started happening as I got well.

BILL: It's important to surround yourself with someone, whether it's a therapist or just a friend, who doesn't think you're crazy. And I'm not saying I believe in Ra.

ANDREW: And I'm not saying that I believe in Ra either. It was some sort of powerful energy that came through.

BILL: But I'm nonplussed by the whole thing. Ra or no Ra, Andrew is Andrew. Andrew has experiences of energy. And you know, this happens to be a convenient symbol and vision, a visual of something. To me, the specifics of Ra aren't important. It's that we all can experience energies. One of the really powerful aspects of this book and of your own journey is that you allow yourself—you allowed, and you're allowing and continue to allow yourself—to experience energies that you were programmed not to accept.

ANDREW: That's right.

BILL: As you mentioned several times, your programmed self said get away from the Love King, get away from Kamala, these people are not part of my reality, they're going to take me down the wrong path. You're confronting this all over again, but you're not running away from Ra. It's like, hey, Ra doesn't really fit into my everyday reality, but he showed up, he's got something he wants to convey, or she, or whatever the energy is, and insofar as you allow yourself to just play it out, you will achieve integration.

ANDREW: Yes. An important factor that I realized eventually was that I had to drop my interpretation of what was happening. I do my best not to interpret the experience through wild guesses or through previous filtered conditioned beliefs.

BILL: Well, every time you do that, it's kind of like, oh, I've got a quick solution, I wrap it up, and then I don't have to deal with it.

ANDREW: It keeps me out of the unknown if I do it that way. I try my best to learn to flow in the unknown and rest in the unknown, and get comfortable with being uncomfortable, and that has allowed me to experience more, and allowed for deeper integration to occur within me; a much more grounded centeredness of how I navigate life because of that. With this experience today, it's also a joint experience with my girlfriend with whom I continue to do healing work, psychotherapy work. We are on a path of—which I find is always humorous to me—that the more we do this healing work or psychotherapy work, we're supposed to be moving toward less crazy, but these experiences seem to be more crazy for me and my journey. I use those words lightly, "more crazy," that the healthier we get, the wilder reality actually is. The deeper we go, the more unknown it actually is. It's hard to put it in a box. This has been my experience. The journey may be different for others.

BILL: I wrote a book many years ago called *How to Test Your Own Mental Health*, and the definition of mental health was adaptability. So, the healthier you become, the more adaptable you become, and the more you're going to be able to integrate the unexpected, unusual, wild reality, that is the true reality in which we exist. Most of human civilization is about slowing down reality so that it becomes predictable because it feels safe. But when you are truly empowered, you don't need that protection, and you can experience all of reality, which is far more unexpected and unpredictable.

Being comfortable with the unknown is not easy. For many people, it's not possible at all. This is a very good example, for you as well as for the readers, of the healthier you get, the more challenges will arise. I see this experience with Ra today is a challenge pushing you to a higher level of centeredness. Who knows what's going to happen with your next client. You may need this.

ANDREW: It's true, many of my own direct experiences, my clients come through with something similar as they deepen their own inner work. They seem to have similar experiences. You're right, it's like my own experiences are there for me to learn and to bring through to my own work to support and guide others. I also agree with what you're saying, the ability to bounce back—adaptability, the word you used—I feel that is a huge component to what I call well-being, and having that ability to bounce back from stressful situations, whether it's relationships, some-thing happens at work, or a Ra shows up in your life, it's having that ability to bounce back and to be with what's arising, to be with the unknown, is a huge ingredient in ongoing well-being.

BILL: In the next chapter, we're going to talk about well-being versus happiness, and why well-being is a better indication of health than the experience of happiness. It doesn't mean you shouldn't enjoy happiness, but in terms of a goal, well-being is a more practical goal to seek, and a more useful goal, because when you're in a state of well-being, you're going to be able to deal with the unexpected and the unknown. When you're in a state of happiness, you can get thrown out of happiness just by something going wrong around you.

ANDREW: I find that in my experience with a growing foundation of well-being, that happiness and true joy arises naturally out of that, and it shows up and is more sustained each day.

BILL: You can feel solid whether someone you love has just died; whether you yourself have just had an accident, you can still have a sense of well-being. It's hard when these things happen to necessarily feel happy—they are not happy moments—but you can still have a sense of well-being. Whereas if you seek happiness, you can be in a euphoric state and the smallest thing, you have a minor car accident, all of a sudden your happiness disappears because now you must deal with, oh my gosh, the insurance, and the other driver's irate, but you can still have a sense of well-being. I didn't get killed. Things are okay. We'll deal with it. And you go forward.

So, in the next chapter, let's talk more about happiness. *Happy For No Reason* is a bestseller, and *The Happiness Principles*. There's been all this focus on happiness. There is nothing wrong with all that. But I think that people can really benefit from a chapter that focuses on what is well-being and how you can achieve it, maintain it, and some of the techniques that you have developed on your own that assist people in finding a sense of well-being.

ANDREW: Holding tightly onto expectations can be a happiness drain. It's okay to show up with an expectation, however for me real life is all about being directly with what is. Agreements are far more powerful than having expectations of others. Agreements allow for participation instead of trying to force others or ourselves to show up in an expected way. We place many expectations on life, people, and ourselves causing so much unnecessary disappointment. Learning to fully let go of our expectations allows for magic to flow, allows for joy to flow. For me, letting go of my expectations and understanding the power of agreements over expectations was a powerful step forward into greater well-being and flow in my everyday experience.

CHAPTER EIGHT

WELL-BEING AND WELL-DOING

BILL: In chapter seven, we started to explain the difference between well-being and happiness. Andrew, explicate, with some examples, why well-being is a more achievable goal, and more importantly, a more important goal for us to pursue.

ANDREW: My experience is that well-being is a non-static state that was always there in the background hidden underneath all of my previous experiences in life; it is [everyone's] natural, embodied, core state of being. If everything goes right, as we grow and develop, well-being becomes the baseline as we navigate the world. If things don't go as planned as we grow up, which happens to many of us whether we know it or not, later in life we actually have a huge capacity to repair those ruptures and integrate missed developmental experiences, moving us into greater levels of well-being. It seems to be the natural state for everyone at the center of all the life storms we encounter. Well-being, to me, contains a felt sense of embodied safety on all levels of my being, a feeling that everything is deeply okay in the world. It's a feeling of being fully integrated through my system, resting in the entire body, with my full personality online, operating from the social engagement system (not the fight or flight system), feeling connected to the planet, to the people around me, and to the collective. For me, when I'm hanging out in deep well-being, it feels like a warm bubbly bliss in the body. I like to call it the internal hot tub.

When we learn to open as Awake Awareness, the unconditioned state, well-being begins to arise from underneath all the conditioning and storms, bringing our system into a more optimal balance. Through right action designed for each individual's unique needs, anyone can move into greater well-being by repatterning and incrementally rewiring their entire system, balancing their body, mind, and energy using cultivated tools like Awake Awareness, healing, working with experts, effortless or deliberate mindfulness, and behavioral changes. It takes commitment and it doesn't have to be hard. Awake Alignment, when online, will continue to guide us to exactly what's needed for our well-being to deepen. Well-being is everyone's birthright and many teachers have also stated that it's our natural state as a human being. They describe it as an experience of a deep relaxed state of being, or a stable ground of being, where there's this natural body bliss, flow, and joy that arises from within all of us. When we drop deeper into this accessible state, life begins to flow more effortlessly and with ease.

For me, when I look at what most of our culture is calling happiness—having things, achievements and people that we desire—this happiness can be tough for everyone to achieve and is fleeting. We get lost in chasing happiness. We get lost in desires that generate ongoing chronic disappointments when we don't achieve what we desire. Seems to me that many people get lost in sadness as they chase happiness. Happy and sad are two sides of the same coin. You can't have one without the other. They are a contrast, like in order to have rich, you must have poor. If we are all the rich, then there is no such thing as the poor.

Compared to well-being, what we label as "happiness" is a passing state that is dependent upon something outside of us. Like all emotions, different levels of the state happiness rise and fall throughout our experiences, and it seems to be conditional and impermanent. I was taught that if I achieve my goals, I could be happy, or if I find that girl who I've been looking for I can find happiness. I ended up in a lot of sadness chasing after what I was told would make me live in an ongoing state of happy. This never-ending pursuit of this temporary promise was a trap I got unknowingly stuck in.

Chasing happiness can quickly descend into sadness or disappointment without a solid foundation of well-being to rest back into. I feel this chase can never end when we are stuck in the trap of conditioned desire. When we feel lack, we chase happiness fueled by desires. Lack action just fuels more lack. Fear action creates more fear. Expanding our awareness, then taking well-doing action from a state of well-being generates more well-being in our life. I move toward aligned right action to increase my well-being for that reason. The quality of the energy behind that action is what matters. To me, the energy and intention that powers my action matters even more than the action taken. What you put out into the universe is what you get back. Generating more well-being feels really important with that understanding of how this reality seems to operate.

I also feel that experiencing a wide range of emotions, from happiness and sadness to anger, is a very natural human experience. You can experience a beautiful full range of emotions while resting in a foundation of well-being.. Through right aligned action and right guidance, we can integrate deeper levels of well-being into our everyday life. We can remain unshakeable and stable while the beauty, energy, storms and chaos of life swirl all around us each day.

BILL: How does one achieve a state of well-being? On the one hand, it seems very natural that as long as you're being fed and properly cared for you have a state of well-being from birth, and yet, very few individuals reach adulthood able to create a sense of well-being on a daily basis.

ANDREW: That's true. Being fed and properly cared for I believe is every human being's birthright. Having our basic human needs met is important and a really great start. Just those needs being met doesn't necessarily result in a stabilized state of well-being in everyday life while operating with a natural, ongoing, felt sense of confidence and safety in the world. When we grow up through our development, if everything goes smoothly, typically we will operate in the world feeling safe, feeling confident, and secure in our relationships. With attuned caregivers, it will be imprinted into us through our healthy childhood developmental experiences that the world is a safe place and we are safe. This results in a confident person who will be more likely to feel satisfied and excited to chase their dreams and passions from a state of well-being and abundant action leading to abundance in all areas of life, from relationships to finances to career and overall satisfaction.

Some of us may believe everything went smoothly when we actually missed out on many important developmental childhood experiences that generate healthy adult behaviors, an open sense of safety in connection, and proper nervous system and biological functioning that help us feel well-being and act in well-doing ways. We are all impacted in different ways and may not even notice it. For some of us, it could be something as simple as a caregiver doing too much for us or maybe not enough for us, both of which could be ongoing misattunements. It could even be having a caregiver with a consistently anxious nervous system, always signaling to us that something is wrong in life. This signal can easily become our own template for how we view the world and its been with us for so long that we just don't realize what is causing this state of chronic unhappiness. Even early childhood illness can have huge negative impacts on our well-being and create ruptures that require repair for optimal and easefull functioning in the world.

As we grow up, many of us are told that in order to feel good, we need to look outside of ourselves, we need to achieve, we need to land the job, have the money, create a certain life, and then in some future time, we're going to feel good, we're going to feel fulfilled. That's never the case. Now is all there is. Future fulfillment is a trap. Through right action and learning to feel great in the Now allows for us to move on to a path that is paved with even greater depths of well-being. From there, opportunities and things seem to easily come our way. Most of us always seem to be chasing the carrot on the end of the stick in hopes of some sort of relief or false happiness. Well-being is a warmth in our very core whenever we are in balance. We may have to unlearn and reconstruct our reality so we can create an internal state of well-being which, in turn, creates a reality of well-being outside of ourselves. For me, I look at my life like I'm going to the well-being gym now. I think, "How can I increase my internal capacity to feel good and feel well-being?" I also train my clients at the well-being gym that fits their own unique needs and journey.

Through this path, through the years of doing healing work, therapy work, attachment work and all these different trainings, I've realized that each one of us has only a certain level of well-being we can handle and take in where we currently are. To my surprise, I found out we all actually have limits to how good we can have life. When we hit our ceiling we some-times sabotage it all or run from it. If we choose, we can learn our lessons through love instead of fear and with commitment to the well-being gym, make our well-being ceilings our new floor and continue to climb up. Many of us are actually afraid of well-being and not even aware of it. Peter Cummings, the attachment genius who created the Adult Attachment Repair Model, who I've trained and worked with for years, has done many years of in-depth field research on the human attachment system, healing work, and understanding our bonding process. He is brilliant. He taught me a lot about the human system and how to heal our deepest wounds. He gave me insight into my own fear of well-being and how much I was able to handle at a time. He also taught me how to increase my capacity to handle internal well-being which then translates to external well-being. My wealth, relationships, health, and easefulness in life continually grow as I integrate more and more well-being.

I've learned that during our development and through the process and stages of our bonding experiences with our primary caregiver, we form a certain level of well-being and capacity to sustain it. Many factors come into play, including what's passed down through lineage. Peter discovered, through supporting thousands of people [as they] repair their attachment system, that many people actually freak out at some point during the get-ting well process and go into fear and struggle when they feel good. We hear about people sabotaging things that are good in their life. Sabotage can be another way a fractured part uses a behavior to try to protect the system from pain and overwhelming emotion. This is a reenactment of their past pain and suffering. This past pain and suffering feels safe and familiar to these parts.

Reenactment happens to many people without them even realizing they are unconsciously recreating their own pain and suffering in the world. There are times it may not be reenactment, but this happens more than we realize. It can also be a way to remain in control, to keep the familiar chronic disappointment ongoing in life. Disappointment may be what we knew all our lives, to our system this feels safer than the feel goods. Our system would rather keep us safe than feel good at times. Our human animal will forfeit love for safety and our soul will forfeit safety for love. The soul and the animal need each other to navigate reality. Bringing these two parts of our self into integration is an important step to living a fully awake life. Our human attachment system seems to connect all these parts together when functioning optimally for the environment we are in. Understanding the attachment system and repairing it seems necessary for well-being.

It's important to understand that there are parts of us that focus only on survival. Learning to work with these parts of us can be of great benefit when we are interested in deeper levels of well-being and flow in life. Feeling good is unfamiliar to some of us, so it may be unsafe to those parts invested in our survival. We have to generate safety and teach these protectors and parts that it's safe to feel good. And we cannot convince them. They must be shown and proven time and time again through ongoing incremental experiences that support us into new depths of well-being in our everyday life. If we look around we can see evidence of this playing out in many people's lives. When people start to achieve a level of success and they start to feel good, they tend to blow those things up or sabotage them, either unconsciously or consciously, because it's too good.

Peter also calls this—I always like hearing him say something like, "the other shoe to drop syndrome"—when things are becoming really good and safe in life, some of us start to panic, and we feel like something bad might happen, because that's a lot of our experiences as children growing up in this world. We start to feel really good, and then it gets taken away from us in unattuned ways. We begin to not trust life. If we want to feel good, then we have to grow our capacity to feel good. We have to grow our capacity to feel and rest in a state of well-being, and we have to feel safe while feeling good. There doesn't seem to be a quick fix yet like we all would like. I am open to that. We can accelerate this process through right action and commitment to ourselves.

As we move forward, getting to know our internal systems, we will encounter parts that have been isolated inside of our system. These parts can be unintentionally blocking our well-being. They are created through traumatic experiences or ongoing, scary, overwhelming experiences. Parts will create or call in protectors that are the gatekeepers to our vulnerable fractured parts. Protectors come in all forms of behaviors, personality traits, energies and are extremely intuitive to support with finding safety or getting needs met. A protector could be a manager part that likes to stay really busy to distract from overwhelming emotions or discomfort. In order for us to deepen into well-being, we need to understand that protectors are powerful and will not allow anyone in without knowing it's safe. They will only accept authentic love, attunement, and acceptance. Learning to work with parts and protectors in ourselves and others can greatly increase our access to the state of well-being and can help us return back to well-being if we lose our connection to it.

BILL: One of the other important components is guilt. It's not just that the other shoe is going to drop. It's that too often, people who are experiencing joy, happiness, and well-being feel guilty because others are not. How do you prepare yourself so that you can retain compassion, which is a positive, but not feel guilt, which interferes with your own sense of well-being?

ANDREW: As our well-being grows our success in life grows. We can feel like we are doing something wrong, no longer living with the world in pain. Guilt to me in this context seems to be a way for our system to keep us connected to the collective, which is another potential survival strategy. Continuing to deepen well-being is a medicine for this. When we feel confident, safe, and secure in ourselves, we can let others have their experience without it impacting us in negative ways. We show deep compassion for them without taking on their projections and pain. When you realize your worth as a divine spark, then guilt seems to drop away in life. It's also common in our world that we see misery being more celebrated than success. If someone sees somebody being successful, there can be jealousy or animosity toward that person. There's a lot of comparison, a lot of competition out there.

Social media is a great example. It could be used as an amazing tool for connection, but it seems to generate comparison and lack, creating more separation than connection these days. The energy behind shares and posts, I notice, seems to come from lack or predatory marketing. It doesn't seem like a lot of people get excited for each other when they have success. Many people just seem to be going through preprogrammed motions, not even aware they may be operating in survival safety strategies.

We can get stuck in our safety strategies that we have been using since we were children to protect ourselves and to defend ourselves from feeling overwhelmed. These strategies include conditioning ourselves to fit in, so we feel safe within the collective, within humanity. We try to orient ourselves to find safety using our gifts or take actions to fill voids and get needs met any way we can. If we are running these strategies—which some use the term character structures—we may be disconnected from our bodies, disconnected from our true Self, and living in separation in the world. We are closed off and not fully living in our authentic expression or Awake Alignment. These strategies mean well and actually played an important role in us surviving. They are out of date and no longer need to be running all the time.

Emotions, like feeling guilty for feeling good, are usually connected to these safety strategies. Guilt can, at times, be used in one of the strategies to return back to safety. When we can find a greater self-awareness of when we're running these programs, these old operating systems for safety, we can begin to work with them, update the protectors, integrate them, and let them go. Letting them go has to be approached with kindness, agendaless love, and attunement to get to the core rupture to integrate and repair.

When we encounter a protector or defense in ourselves or others, it's helpful to fully understand the world the protector was created in. We can all easily learn a process to work with our parts to find a deeper integration of ourselves. Allowing a person to speak from the protector and understand what that part really needs creates an opportunity for the missed experience to be brought to the light of awareness, whether it's safety or another need. We can then support the person in getting what they needed until the defense finally lets go for love to fully meet the vulnerable part. Listening with agendaless love and allowing for the natural releasing of the protection and strategy is important, whether we're working in support of ourselves or another.

Forcing or trying to will through the process in any way will generally tighten the grip of the defense and generate more resistance. Through releasing our safety strategies, we can open back up and connect back to essence, embodying it into the world. When we're embodied, feeling safe with our hearts open, well-being is our natural state. It begins to flow freely throughout our systems. When we create positive practices, through self-awareness, character structure maps, and through becoming aware of what we're using to protect ourselves when we feel unsafe, we can become present with what is and orient back into our Awake Alignment.

Going to the well-being gym is important to strengthen new pathways of well-being and create practices that identify and release defenses, old habits of self, and outdated behavior causing separation and generating ongoing unnecessary suffering. We can create internal well-being, as well as external well-being. Lately, I've been looking at ways of how I can increase my human user experience of my life to create greater well-being externally as well as internally.

BILL: Give some examples of what you do externally to create an inner sense of well-being.

ANDREW: Throughout my journey, I've developed and stabilized deeper levels of internal well-being which has created more abundant well-being action with each action I take. There's a greater momentum to those actions, generating a greater return of well-being and balance in my life. What you put out into the world you get back. The most important thing is not the actual action, it's what is at the core powering each action; the quality of the energy behind the action at the baseline of your system.

Through each abundant action I take that has been sourced from deeper levels of well-being over what we call time, I have created a successful easeful business where I now get to support others on their journey. I've reached a new level of abundance that I was not able to acquire from the level of well-being access I had in the past. A new level that I was unable to manifest into my life previously naturally showed up, with this new baseline level of well-being. Without doing my own internal work, I wasn't able to maintain and keep this reality stable in the past. Now I can. This new abundance has afforded me the ability to start looking at well-being in my external reality—meaning, what can I do outside myself that can begin to create more ease and the greatest sense of well-being?

Recently, I went on a trip and at the airport I realized I was struggling rolling this old suitcase I had had for years. It was this tiny suitcase, the wheels were all kind of jacked up on it. When I was rolling it, it would go way left instead of straight. I'm running through the airport trying to get to my plane, and this suitcase is dragging awkwardly behind me, slowing me down and twisting my wrist. I'm like, this is terrible. Why am I not buying a new suitcase? Because I'm so used to this old lifestyle where I have to save and not purchase items that are not absolutely necessary. I was still living from this old passed down idea that I need to sacrifice the things that could make life better for me, in order to survive. Then it dawned on me that I could actually go out and buy a new suitcase. My old mentality was to go to Marshalls, go to some place that has second-hand suitcases, which is okay, nothing wrong with that, but I was like, you know what, I'm going to really look into this and I'm going to take care of myself in a way I never had.

I went to Bloomingdale's to buy a suitcase. The prices were outlandish, according to my old lens of seeing reality. I shopped around these suitcases and I was trying them out at Bloomingdale's feeling all luxurious. I couldn't believe how smooth these things were and how amazingly they were rolling. This experience opened my eyes to life upgrades, and how easy your life can be by rolling a suitcase that is made by a company that actually pays attention to the details. Now when I looked into it, this company pays so much attention to detail all the way down to the grip experience. When you're holding the grip of the handle of the suitcase, the user experience there is really soft and convenient; it feels really good on the hand and wrist. The comfort is obvious. As I roll it, it's so smooth and easy to roll. My whole traveling life has changed in a way that I never thought or ever could have imagined. It was a simple change. A simple external life upgrade that can add up with each moment of use.

What ignited this change is a friend of mine was showing me this car that he owns, this beautiful Porsche. I drive a Ford Fusion. He showed me his experience, the finer details they put into this car. He's having me go over and open and close the door. He showed me how the handle feels, how the door makes a certain sound. The level of care and love they put into the details of this car really creates an amazing user experience. So, I started thinking why not find simple ways to create an amazing user experience for all my life? And that's how this whole thing with the suitcase came along. I really love going on trips now. My travel experiences really have changed so much from this simple shift. I get excited to pack my suitcase and actually use it. In the past, I never had any joy whatsoever with a suitcase. Now I love it. It's amazing.

BILL: Well, this is interesting because the very first title we were considering to use for this book was Do, Be, Do. And you're thinking about Do, then Be, and Well-Be. Because it's not just about do, be, do, be; it's do well, be well, do well, well-being. So, it's interesting in this particular instance you're citing examples of doing that are based on a higher awareness of what and why you're doing. There's nothing wrong with spending five or even ten times as much, whether it be for a car, a suitcase, or any other element if, one, you can afford it, and two, it gives not just joy of the moment, but contributes to a greater sense of well-being within the person. I think that's the key that you've explained in your example of the luggage.

ANDREW: That's right. I can now see that in the past, instead of well-doing I was pain-doing. Living in pain, taking action from that quality of energy creating more pain for myself. Then, through right action, I transitioned into well-being. Now I'm doing from well-being, so I'm well-doing. What that looks like is that the source or the quality behind the action I'm taking is more from abundant loving action. I naturally began to care about my external well-being. I'm now acting from a place of self-love that creates an upgraded user experience or an upgraded kinder experience for my physical body—its greater ease on my body, my hand; the suitcase itself is of great ease. Flying is so much easier. It creates an overall sense of well-being externally and it's coming from a source of energy that's within me of love and care for my experience on this planet. It's not coming from lack or a hole or void I'm trying to fill; I'm just upgrading my state of internal well-being. I call this more abundant action or abundant doing, or well-doing. This ease will translate to greater kindness and more ease in my relationship, health, and emotional well-being. This small shift will ripple through my entire life and these types of incremental micro well-being actions quickly add up.

BILL: What's interesting in your example is you're also connecting to the energy and the intentionality of those who have created these conveniences, whether it be luggage or car, of greater joy. It harkens back to our most immediate bestseller, which is *The Life Changing Magic of Tidying*

Up—does it spark joy? What you've explained is that what is created in joy does spark joy. Maintaining a connection throughout the energetics of what went into the idea behind creating something—the care, the details as you call them, of the creation—automatically connects with you at your higher vibratory rate, which is really the goal of everything we've been talking about.

The state of well-being is a state of high vibration which does not allow for temporary obstacles to invade and change in a systematic way your true nature. Unfortunately, for most human beings, their systems, if they started out in a state of well-being, have been infiltrated by the lower vibratory energy, whether it be fear, whether it be violence, or just unpleasantness, that actually has interfered with their ability to remember what that state of well-being is, and to recreate that state. For those who have not had the good fortune of non-experience of the negative, which is just about everyone, what do you recommend for your clients to overcome these recurring programmings that take away from the ability to experience well-being?

ANDREW: One of the things I recommend is to understand that this is a process and it doesn't seem to ever be an overnight thing. There's a possibility it could be an overnight thing, but I haven't experienced that or met anyone who has achieved that yet. When I look at my experience, I see myself as a cumulative energy field of all my past experiences adding up to this current moment right here, right now. My current energy that I'm vibrating out of my being has been incrementally created, moment by moment, over what we are calling time.

If you look at an empty glass and begin to fill it with grains of sand, one by one, each grain representing a grain of new experience, eventually that glass will fill up and we agree that this full glass has been incrementally filled up, and that could be a way to look at what we are in form. If someone came over and looked at the glass when it was full, they may think that's how it's always been. It was a process for that glass to be there in that form, for that glass to fill up to that exact amount of full. Incremental experiences had in moments over time adding up and filling up a container that's then vibrating at a certain energy. That was a process. Life is a process. What I am in this form is a process, not static. It was over many, many experiences.

If we are in a state of pain, a state of non well-being, and we're afraid of well-being and we're vibrating at that level, it's helpful to understand that reversing that process is incremental. We get to be kind and compassionate, understanding that we need to begin to create new experiences, internally and externally, that add up incrementally over time to create greater levels of well-being. It's never static. We can consciously generate new experiences with the support of others by free will choice to create a new field of vibration. We're a verb, not a noun. We're always changing, shifting and growing and evolving moment by moment. Always new each moment. During this process of moving into greater well-being, it can be different for everybody. Our individual level of self-awareness is important. It's important to strengthen self-awareness to deepen compassion and raise our energy vibration for what we find.

There are a lot of healing modalities and ways to get support. There are many books, guides, awake teachers and many other things out there that can begin to support us in stepping into greater levels of well-being. I started without many resources and found I was guided because of my pure intention to get well and discover who I am. But a quick start is to increase self-reflecting awareness. Understanding the self, realizing our true nature, is the most important realization in my opinion, because the more expansive and deeper the awareness we have, then we know where to go and what to do. We can learn to flow in an Awake Aligned right action, or course correct back into alignment with acceptance and life tools as needed. We can begin to listen to the inner guidance of our Awake Alignment, our pure unconditioned essence, which has its own guidance system to get back into balance. Back on course.

This universe seems to always want to get back into balance. Same thing with humans, the human body, seeming to always want to get back to homeostasis, back into balance. If we can have a level of self-awareness where we can listen to that guidance, we're going to be internally guided to things that will help build more and more experiences over time to create higher and deeper levels of stable well-being within us, within our system. Many of my clients come to me as if they're coming to the energy gym, and we're working out well-being together, and they get results, gains over time, where their lives begin to shift because the internal is a reflection of the external. The greater levels of well-being we can handle, the more joy, the more abundance, the more ease, the more fun we can have. The more things we want and didn't even know we wanted come to us effortlessly. Things seem to work themselves out. When things hit us in our system that are stressful, experiences that are stressful, the faster we can bounce back. Learning what we need and committing to well-being is a choice and a must if we want to flow into more easeful effortless manifestation. We can choose to learn through that or we can choose to learn through something else. It's a free will choice and our true intentions set it all in motion.

BILL: One of the good points to end this chapter with is just as rarely can you achieve well-being overnight, it doesn't matter where you are in your process, because it is a process, you're likely to achieve positive results over time. It's never too late to start, no matter what your present circumstances. Is that what you find with your clients?

ANDREW: Yes, I have. I think that you could be at any age, any place, any time, you can begin to add well-being. I like to look at my life as more than just this life. Starting now, at any time or age, makes sense for other lives you may have as well; what we may think of as the future. You can easily begin right now in this moment by shifting your awareness to something that's going right in your life. If you have a roof over your head, if you have some food, wherever you're sitting, if you're breathing. If you shift your awareness just to notice these little things, you'll start to build incremental experiences of well-being. You don't have to force yourself into gratitude, you don't have to force yourself into all of these forced practices. It's just a shift of awareness onto positive levels, or positive aspects of reality. There are ways of simply doing that in every moment. At night, I like to do a day review of all the good that flowed to me. I fill a page in a book of the blessings I have. I feel a deep sense of gratitude for all these amazing blessings and how lucky I am to have all that I've been given. To live where I live and to be given the freedom to explore this work. I am amazed at how much I have and how blessed I am to just be breathing.

BILL: The last topic for this chapter, we spoke a little bit about the concept of space, and how space is related to a sense of well-being. Explain what you mean when you talk about space and its connection to well-being.

ANDREW: There are many different ways to approach this topic, but one of the things I find to be true is that space is absolutely necessary in all areas of life. If we get too fused or fixated in an experience, we can get lost in the experience. Con-fused can become our state when we get fused in experiences for too long. If we get overwhelmed, stuck, or have a lot of overwhelming grief, sadness, or pain while being so fixated and focused on that, we may actually be fueling energy into it or keeping it stuck and unprocessed within us. We can loop in a pain loop. So, it takes up some space inside us, drains us of energy.

There are ways we can shift our awareness into a spacious view or vantage point, which allows for a greater quality of space in our body and mind. Space consciousness or awareness can be found outside the body or deep within. Depending on the energetic constitution of someone, out or in may be the doorway to this quality of consciousness. Spaciousness from experience allows for us to not get lost in our everyday mind content and supports the release of contraction and tension. I feel Eckhart Tolle is pointing to this quality of consciousness in *The New Earth*, about space consciousness. Some people say we're mostly made up of empty space—using those words to me is a little confusing; I feel we are way more than just empty space. Space is not actually empty. This is just a pointer to an experience that anyone can realize. I feel we have an aspect of us that is spacious, that is free from content and form. By learning to rest our awareness in this quality of space consciousness, we can create more space within the body, within the system, allowing energy to flow and eventually allow greater well-being to flow. Spaciousness or open awareness allows us internal room to process and integrate experiences.

If you want to feel greater depths of pleasure and excitement, we have to have the capacity to have space around all experiences so it can flow through us, so we can have that full experience instead of cutting off, stopping it, or blocking or contracting around it. Fear contracts us, chronic fear creates chronic tension. Fear can cut off life, reducing energy flow, well-being, and overall health. Space is a component to what we are, it's a part of what we are, and when we can integrate space into our lives, it creates greater well-being and greater levels of excitement, joy and pleasure as well.

BILL: Space is the one true element for both doing and being. You can't do outside of space, but you also can't be outside of space.

ANDREW: Spacious awareness allows for a bird's eye view of life and our experiences allowing our true identity to not get lost in the world. When we rest in the spacious aspect of consciousness, it opens our system, reducing contraction in the body, allowing for an increase of the flow of energy throughout our system where we will eventually empty out "content" and liberate our experience into the stillness and realization of the "emptiness" aspect of all things.

Content, when viewed spaciously and focused on from this higher vantage point, will lead to an emptying out until we rest into the empty spacious witnessing self allowing us not to continually get lost in stories, looping, or life drama from here. Some of us have easy access to it, some of us may need pointers to it. Once realized, it can be deepened as can all aspects of the field of consciousness. Intimate awareness, another quality aspect of the field of consciousness, allows us to be with our life experience and content with compassion, warmth, attunement, and kindness. Some of us have easy access to that quality of consciousness, some of us may need pointers to that.

Again, once realized it can be deepened. Combining spaciousness and an intimate quality to life without fusing to our experiences and confusing our true identity, we can feel, be with, and even at times deeply enjoy. When you approach life from a spaciousness, intimate compassionate pure empty awareness, with an open heart, feeling safe, connected, and grounded while walking embodied in the world, orienting to our authentic core values, this is Awake Alignment. This Awake Alignment allows the flow of dynamic, intelligent, creator energy, generating expansive flow states that guide our natural wisdom intelligence to heal, discern situations to apply right action, and generate creative spiritual power magnetically bringing to us all we need to operate in internal and external states of well-being with authentic power to have a loving impact on all that we choose to experience in life. Integrating these levels of our system and being can begin right Now or deepen while accelerating the process with right action while honoring divine timing. It does not have to be hard. It does not have to be hard. We are all being supported in this. We are being gently guided to come back to alignment, to come back home to rest in the warmth of our birthright, our natural state of well-being.

CHAPTER NINE
INTEGRATING THE SYSTEM

BILL: Transformative integration. So, we ended the last chapter with the discussion of the difference between well-being and happiness, and this chapter goes a little deeper. True well-being requires a level of integration that is actually transformative. Andrew, explain what you mean when you talk about integration and why integration is not static, but transformative.

ANDREW: When I look back on my path thus far, I started off this journey with the intention to heal myself and to feel better. Using therapy, personal development tools, and mindfulness were some of the ways that I approached this. And it did work, you know, the things I did supported me in feeling a greater level of well-being relative to where I was; I started to feel better as I continued my commitment to this work.

Over time, as I've shared a little bit of this path, my journey opened up into an unexpected journey. I never planned to find magic on the way and I needed to be ready for it. Each exploration, each healing experience kept leading me deeper into a world I never knew existed or even thought was possible. We are infinitely complex beings, however, there are different levels of our systems in this reality that we can integrate and balance, so we can live into our greatness.

Each step along my path, consciousness taught me about different qualities of consciousness, states of awareness or mind, and different levels and parts of the human system that play important roles in our personal realities and how we create those realities. I was missing access to parts of my system that I required to be online and functioning properly for me to do the work I came here to do on this planet and in this life. Understanding myself and all the different levels, from my mental, cognitive, emotional, energetic and physical experiences, was necessary to get me out of these life loops, repeating trauma patterns, and to locate in me where I needed to do some work to upgrade and integrate those aspects of my system to work at their optimal level.

As this process unfolded with my focus on myself, my life naturally began to change effortlessly on its own for the better. Up until then, I felt stuck in most of my life experiences, as many others are lost in certain levels of what we think reality is. Throughout my journey into the territory of work with myself and through the work I do with others, I realized that we have all these different amazing parts of our systems. We have the mind, the body, we have emotions, we have logic, soul, and so forth, there's more, and a lot of it is un-integrated, and a lot of us get stuck in certain parts of our system.

Many people have mapped it out in many different ways. Many of us are stuck in only our bodies, our minds, or our emotions, in ordinary everyday consciousness. We also have the soul level, energy, or the subtle body and subtle mind, which is another level of our system we can all experience and stabilize. Sometimes we can get stuck here in energy. There are different terms people use for these qualities of reality. And then there's what people point to as Non-Dual, Awake Awareness or Spirit, divine mind or an awake pure knowing state. So, each one of these different parts of the system can be realized, we can awaken to it through direct experience, become aware of these parts of the system, these qualities of reality that are always here.

We can locate where we're blocking the integration from occurring or causing unnecessary suffering or pain through unprocessed trauma in the system. Many of us have a backlog of trauma and painful experiences that our system would like to digest and release, but it needs to be in its optimal functioning for it to do that. When we feel unsafe or in fear, our system may be fully closed or partially closed, not allowing for processing or integration to occur.

Optimal functioning is when our system is available to receive and process new information, allowing us to release old information, while keeping the lessons and gifts, but not the emotional charge or trauma that came along with it. A mentor once told me trauma is pervasive through-out humanity. We seem to have individual and collective trauma that we might not even consider to be trauma. As a collective, we are currently in the process of letting it go.

Having our systems operate optimally will accelerate this and will support us in living in greater well-being, individually and together. My journey was becoming aware of what was needed through using the tool of self-reflective awareness, going to get what I needed, integrating and embodying those qualities and wisdoms and then walking those wisdom qualities into everyday life. We are all at different places on the journey, but I learned that if you begin to integrate heart, mind, body, spirit as a whole, well-being actually begins to increase naturally in your body and life.

The more we integrate our entire system, the better we feel. Well-being also does not seem to be static. It's always changing and shifting. When I look back, first I started with the mental and the mind as a doorway into my system, working on my belief systems, looking at my conditioned beliefs. My awareness expanded. And then I moved to more of the physi-cal, started taking supplements, taking care of my nutrition, working out, doing yoga. And through that process, all of a sudden, something started to shift naturally in my body when my soul came online. My essence started driving the system. Again my awareness expanded.

And then I started doing energy medicine, subtle body integration, energetics, blended with the mental and physical. So, my path was basi-cally a journey of teachings that came through my own experiences of expanding awareness and teachers of how to integrate the full system of heart, mind, body and spirit and live in Awake Alignment, which will open well-being in our lives. There are many doorways, depending on the person and their specific typology or type of system constitution. Any doorway into the system to do this work can be used, or multiple doorways, like mental or emotional, physical, energetic, outward, inward, or non-local awareness. Once we integrate to a certain level, clean up our egos and find the disowned parts that we call shadows and stabilize different wisdom qualities of consciousness in our system, a natural intelligent wisdom takes over our life. Life lives you. We awaken.

BILL: For most people, the concept of integration is sort of stopping and integrating, but the way you've described it, it's more than that. It's actually active doing as part of the integration process.

ANDREW: I see it as there being awake aligned doing or right action we can take in our everyday life to, you know, move more toward integration, or there's action we can take which will move us away from it, like avoiding pain, or having low emotional intelligence, avoiding different parts of ourselves that are hidden in the system and the unconscious. So, we have to make an effort with the intention to begin to integrate these different aspects of the system. So, there is a doing, there's an aligned doing, I would call it, or right action.

BILL: And what are some of the specific aligned doing techniques that were useful to you, and that are useful to your clients today?

ANDREW: Well, we're all at different places on this journey. And you know, some of us might be just starting out, some might be well advanced. One of the things to really begin to look at is where are your strengths and what are you aware of in your own body, your own system. Locate the doorways that are the most accessible to you. Some of the things that can be really helpful are using human maps, learning our specific typology, or defensive character structures or even understanding the different lines of intelligence.

We all have emotional intelligence, physical intelligence, cognitive intelligence and more. These main lines of intelligences that we all have can vary in advancement from person to person. Some of us might be really great in the logic, the mental, there's people that are really good in the emotion. Some of us are really good in the physical line. There's a lot of people at the gym working out, doing yoga, getting physically fit. I notice there's a tendency to avoid the emotional aspects in our culture; we might need to go to emotional gym, and work that part of ourselves out. We can locate the places in our system through mapping it out or using some wonderful maps that others have created to find those places we may need to bring online or to strengthen. Locating the blind spots to accelerate this work can be really fun and beneficial to our well-being and life experiences, like finding healthy relationships.

BILL: What's an emotional gym?

ANDREW: The emotional gym is when we go to a place to work out that line of intelligence in our system. Just like a physical gym, there are places you can go to work out the emotional muscles which play important roles in health, well-being, feeling safe and fulfilled in life. An example would be getting in touch with your emotions in a healthy way, learning how to feel emotions in the body, practicing letting the emotional energy move freely without contracting around it in fear or stopping the flow of emotional energy.

Fully leaning into the experience of emotion and learning how to experience what's going on, whether it feels pleasurable, or might be something we might not want to feel that we might consider or call negative or bad. We need to experience these emotions so they can move through us and not get stuck inside of us. Without fully processing emotions, we can end up repeating experiences over and over again until we learn to process them and let them go.

Processing emotions leads to personal growth, evolution of our system, and a greater capacity to take on larger, more exciting experiences in life. There's a lot more to having a higher emotional intelligence as well. So, we have to re-learn how to feel, some of us. That was a big part of my process. As I started doing the work, I could think about emotion, I could talk about emotion, I could say I was sad, but I wasn't really feeling any of these emotions. I held them down, packed them in, causing a toxic environment in my body, which resulted in a toxic environment in life. If I vibrate toxic, I get back toxic. When I began to vibrate well-being by increasing my emotional flow and processing emotions, I got back more well-being in my life.

BILL: Well, we have physical gyms and we have equipment, we have exercises, and we have personal trainers we can talk to. So, for emotional connection, emotional integration, where do you start?

ANDREW: Well, because I didn't really know where to start when I was doing this, I was trying to learn how to feel, I was reading books about how to feel, then I realized this is not going to work. This is cognitive. I'm taking it in through the mental doorway. We can start there, but we need to move on and deeper into the experience. So, by connecting with people who could show me, I had to work with people who knew how to feel, who can reconnect to the body in a safe way. I worked with certain healers, teachers, and people who could help me out. Working with a coach, healer, or therapist is like having a fitness instructor for the physical body. You can find someone to work out the emotional body, and you will find greater overall health and well-being. We also seem to look younger with greater emotional fluidity in the body. Some people think being emotional is a weakness. This belief is just not true. Having emotions without collapsing and getting lost in them is healthy and necessary for us to truly live life.

BILL: Can you work with people in your everyday life, or do you have to go to a professional?

ANDREW: You can work with the people in your everyday life. We want to do this safely at first. This can be a tender exercise for some of us. Especially when reconnecting to the emotional body, this is more of a sensitive place. We want to feel really safe, safety is a big deal with this. We want to have someone who can be aligned with us, someone who can understand what we are doing and lead us away from getting lost in experiences and offer proper warm attunement, someone with a high intelligence in the emotional line. So for me, the reason I shut down my emotions was because it didn't feel safe to feel growing up, we were taught to be men, not to feel, you know, just everyone, everyone tells us to shut the emotions down. Be a man. Don't feel.

To reconnect these emotions was very vulnerable at first, it can be very vulnerable, so I had to find somebody who I could be really safe with. If I go to someone who may be not really safe or hasn't had any of these experiences, they might cause me to actually shut down more or protectors may be triggered, closing my system. So, I had to find somebody educated who would be a safe place for that. Safety, warm attunement, understanding and care during this process is extremely important. I wouldn't recommend starting with the local DMV teller to share your experiences with. Go to an expert like you would when looking for a physical trainer. Injuries can happen on the emotional body really easily that can cause all sorts of pain. And again, feeling is not weak. It's actually a sign of true strength.

BILL: How does someone find or determine a safe place and a safe person? Seems to me that in most cases it's going to be wiser to find a therapist of some kind.

ANDREW: That's an emotional gym, when you have a therapist that's more of a body therapist or like somatic embodied therapy. Talk therapy can be helpful, but I feel it's limited and slow. I feel you have to go more into mind/body integration, that type of therapy. Emotionally focused therapy is a place you can go. A kind awake healer or coach who understands this work is a great place to look as well. I like to only work with healers with amazing reputations that attended well rounded training programs and do the work themselves.

There are techniques and things you can find online and in books, but when you're reconnecting to emotions, this is a part of the body. It's like you go to a gym and you have a trainer help you out, so you can consider going to, you know, a mind/body coach or someone who has done this work, or a therapist, to be your trainer in the emotional gym. It's the fastest way. We learn from mirroring others. We have mirror neurons in the brain that pick up actions of others around us. We use those when we interact with people or teachers. We actually learn a lot through this reality, through the process of mirroring one another. So, if we get proper mirroring and real time experience from somebody who knows a lot about the emotional body, they will accelerate the work. It speeds it up.

BILL: So, what about from the mental integration?

ANDREW: Well, for the cognitive line, you can go to the cognitive gym. Working with experts and coaches. Trainings and classes. Reading and learning on your own. I like to learn from experience, some of us enjoy that, and others have other ways they like to take in information. An important aspect of the cognitive is reframing and letting go of outdated, limiting beliefs that no longer serve us or may be blocking us from experiencing the reality we want. We are holding onto a lot of old beliefs and old structures that we've been told growing up, so we may see the world from a limited view.

So, going back, and taking the time to find what our core beliefs are, finding the ones that don't serve us, is really important, so that we can release those and upgrade those. Sometimes we are holding onto beliefs from when we were two or three years old. We're seeing the world through those limited views, at, you know, thirty, forty, fifty years old, and we need to upgrade those to find greater well-being, because they might be in direct conflict with what we're experiencing in reality.

So, me, an example of one of the things that I noticed, one of my core beliefs of this reality, is that I am unsupported. That was one belief that I had, that I had to do everything myself. And I didn't realize that was a core belief inside of me. I was taught to be independent, which can be very beneficial; there's a gift there. But if I'm on the range of too much independence, and too much self-reliance, I'm blocking out the support of others. And in this world, we actually work with people all the time. We need others to be successful. We're finding more and more that a lot of success comes from the support of others and to be able to take in that support instead of trying to hold and do everything yourself. So, as I found that core belief, I had to re-pattern that and shift that by first finding this core belief and upgrading it. But I had to discover it first. So, you have to look inside, see what some of your beliefs are, and see how you're viewing the world to discover what's there, to begin to work with that, to reorganize that.

BILL: Well, to sum up some of what you said, transformative integration allows you to access a greater range of your mental, emotional, and even physical awareness. And in so doing, you become more adaptable, you become healthier, in terms of your ability to respond to your environment, and to create your environment. So, what is the difference today, for you, in being significantly more integrated than you were when you started your journey? What are some of the specific signs you can share with your readers to encourage them on this path?

ANDREW: One of the experiences I am having from deeper integration of these parts of my system is whenever I get into any stressful or overwhelming situations, instead of them lasting months or years, I'm able to move through those experiences and get back to well-being or Awake Alignment much faster. So, my bounce back from these stressful situations is much faster, leaving me feeling more connected and living a more optimal life without as much self-sabotage, unnecessary suffering, and fear. I also have noticed many different shifts in all other areas of my life through this integration work. Like just eating food, eating certain foods or desserts, I actually can feel and taste these things on a higher level. So, there's a deeper pleasure and enjoyment of food and experiences. Taking in different experiences with others. I'm connecting deeper in my relationship.

There are actually physical sensations of well-being that I didn't start to experience until I started this journey. I didn't even know we could feel this in the body. I've felt ecstatic states of bliss, I've felt passion, compassion, care, love, flowing through my body as I increased my emotional intelligence. There are all these things I didn't know that I could experience that started to happen through this integration.

Another really cool benefit of doing integration work [is that] we all come in with very specific, unique gifts that our essence wants to use. Whatever way you want to use them on this journey, whether that's a purpose or mission in life, or just to have fun with, these gifts come online and we can use them as allies as opposed to using them as defenses to protect ourselves. An example of this in my life is, I'm really proficient at seeing and tracking energy in the world and people, and wasn't initially aware that I was doing this, but through life, I was tracking people intuitively, seeing in their systems, seeing their belief systems.

I was really good at sales, actually, because of this gift, but had no idea this is what I was doing to connect with people. I also used it to help others get their needs met. So, I was using that gift unconsciously to protect myself. I would always make sure to scan for safety, track people to see their true intentions with high accuracy. I can see their emotions and energy behind the words they said no matter how much they may have tried to hide it. And now that I'm conscious of this gift, and at my level of integration I am feeling safe in the world, I can use it for whatever I want. I've been using it in my client sessions, I use it in everyday life.

With permission, I use it to track different experiences of others to offer reflection to help them integrate more of what they're doing. And this is just one example of the cool gifts, these energetic gifts that I have always had. And we all have different psychic gifts, different gifts that people point to as psychic abilities, intuitive abilities, creative abilities. All this starts to show up more and more when we integrate all the way through the essence, the heart, mind, body and spirit.

BILL: Well, as you describe it, one of the big benefits is you're more fully alive, you're more fully present to all emotions, and to all experiences. You don't block them out. Is there a downside to being more fully alive? Because when negative things are going on, are you also more vulnerable to them?

ANDREW: You feel everything more deeply. So, yes. I wouldn't say it's downside. Based on my old conditioned beliefs, I used to see the world as more black and white, this or that thinking. Negative or positive. And as I worked more of the cognitive line and the belief systems in my system to go along with this integration, it's rare that I judge things as good or bad. Things are just these experiences that I'm having, whether they generate sadness or joy or pleasure or all of those. And me not labeling them as good or bad, or putting a judgment on them, allows them to move through me faster. Allows me to experience to the fullest.

So, I am experiencing things at a greater depth, but they're no longer stuck inside me or stuck in the background. So, they move through me. So even sadness, what I used to consider bad or something I would want to avoid, I actually feel it, and there's a pleasure in feeling this in a way that I am alive, that I get to feel this experience. And I know the other side of this is a duality of happiness. So, without sadness, I wouldn't feel happiness. So, if I'm allowed to feel that depth of sadness, I'm also able to feel that depth of happiness when it shows up. So, I am much more alive. And I don't actually see a downside, from my perspective, from my beliefs, in the way I see the world. We are gifted life. Feeling fully each moment life has to offer is an amazing adventure in itself. Integration allows for magic, depth and love to flow into all areas of our being.

CHAPTER TEN

AWAKEN TO SOUL

BILL: We've been talking about the relationship between the soul and the body. Part of transformative integration is integrating your human experience with your soul, which some people call spirit—Andrew will talk a little bit about the differences between soul and Spirit—but you can't integrate until you awaken. So, one of the first tasks is to awaken your soul, and to understand your soul's purpose. That is only step one. Andrew, explain what you mean when you tell clients they can awaken to their soul?

ANDREW: There is an intense loving fire of the cosmos that burns bright and deep within us all. A unique spark of the divine that has been gifted to each human through the union of Spirit and form. The realization of this, that we are not just our body and mind is an inevitable step for us all on our journey, whether it happens this lifetime or another. As with all realizations that we glimpse, this soul realization can be deepened, integrated and lived passionately into the world. The soul has a lot of power and force to move us through the world. We can integrate this soul energy into our life with our human. Soul, as I am using it here, is another powerful, bright, unique aspect of our being. There are different types of souls like there are different types of personalities. During a meditation, I was shown how the over soul "splits down" through many levels from the One and how there are soul groups and different types of souls or souls rays. A mentor of mine who studies the Trans Himalayan Teachings confirmed this teaching with me a few years after I was shown this. The complexity of it, as with most of our parts, is not easily captured by simple words or just a chapter in a book, but one way I describe it is it's our unique, individual, spiritual, divine nature that moves down to incarnate into form to integrate with our body/mind system. It contains our unique blueprint and records from our travels and experiences through space and time. It's has its own life fire that must be tapped for us to truly live fully and deeply.

Our soul has an agenda, it's our subtle body that wants to inhabit our form body fully, and we can do this by working with our human parts and soul parts, bringing them into union with each other. On my own journey, when I was beginning to reflect on my inner beliefs and on my conditioning, I began to "see" the ego and its conflicting beliefs that were in me, while no longer being identified to them, or fused into them as real. As my awareness grew, and as my consciousness liberated and confused parts began to liberate, my consciousness began to expand naturally. My sense of self expanded into a new level of reality that I hadn't been fully aware of most of my life, which was the soul level of my being.

When you can see your thoughts without getting lost in them or going on the ride with them you can watch them come and go. This is subtle mind or soul awareness. Soul is a more subtle, wider version of self that can now see the everyday mind thought stream without getting lost into it. As I grew through stages of my own inner work, it was as if my identity began to widen and I found this new level, which has been called subtle body/mind or soul. Different terms are used for it by many wisdom traditions, but this is another wider identity, larger than ordinary human everyday consciousness that seems to be within all humans. We can live in our Awake Alignment identifying as our soul with a human personality as we integrate more of our system through healing, meditation and right action that expands and liberates consciousness.

I also sometimes call it the individual essence or soul essence. When I'm working with clients, some have come with conscious access to this level of their being. They may have done work in the past and they've expanded and they've realized soul. Others may need to realize it through pointers or inner work and then stabilize the energy of soul. As you wake up to these different aspects of self, you start to realize that it's not just the human personality and ego running the show, but that there's also the soul level and many levels beyond. We can continue to widen and grow and become aware of these higher levels of our being through reflective awareness and inner work. And it's in all of us; everybody has these different levels. One of the benefits of these realizations is that as we widen our identity, fear decreases at the greater levels of our being. Suffering is greatly reduced and we have a deeper connection to our purpose and own truth of why we are on our individual journey.

BILL: What are some of the techniques that you specifically used or experienced to realize the difference between your human personality self and your soul self?

ANDREW: One of the key things for me was sitting and reflecting on my inner self from an Awake Alignment. As I became more aware of these thoughts, belief systems, and parts within me, I began to realize that's not what I am, and who I am, and they started to release and liberate through that and healing work. Reflective awareness, without judgement, has the power to see what we once thought was us, what we were once fused into. By seeing what we once thought was a real identity looking through an Awake Alignment, it loosens its power it may have had over us and eventually it dissolves. As these identities and beliefs dissolve, our energy and awareness increases and our consciousness expands, naturally expanding our identity until we fully realize the truth of what we are. As I operated more from soul I began to remember more of my soul purpose and why I journeyed here. I could remember what some call past lives or other experiences my soul had, not from this life. The more I healed and used reflection the more I was fully operating as soul. Soul healing work like letting go of stuck past lives is also another beautiful way to let go of unnecessary suffering. I've seen many examples of people holding onto experiences not of this life that are negatively impacting their health or reality, who have healed those soul experiences. Once they did this, right away their current realities drastically changed for the better when this soul life was healed and integrated. So finding ways to integrate and realize soul has many positive benefits that can shift our realities for the better.

BILL: So, would you call this meditation?

ANDREW: Yes, you can call it meditation. It's an effortless non-doing. Just being quality. Learning to be in an open expansive awake aware state of being reflecting on what's arising will rapidly, naturally let the things go which are false in us if our awareness doesn't get lost on the rides of what's showing up in our field of experience. If we go on a thought ride, that is going down thought trains and visions, we just thank it, and without judgement return back to being in self-reflective open awareness to what's arising. Keep it simple. Don't try to do it or force it. Showing up is all the doing that's needed. Once you show up, then you stop the doing.

BILL: So, basic technique one: meditation.

ANDREW: And self-reflection practices can be really helpful, perhaps journaling. You can self-reflect through journaling. Like in the reflective awareness practice, when our Awake Awareness realizes something by seeing it, our identity to that begins to drop away. Freeing us. How can we be what we can see? Whatever is doing the seeing and experiencing must be more truly us then what we see.

BILL: Technique number two: journaling.

ANDREW: There's working with an integrated coach, an awake healer, or holistic therapist. These can rapidly speed this process up. Learning what your Awake Alignment feels like or how to shift into it by working with someone that can point the way I feel is one of the best things you can do to live from well-being, integrate the system and realize all these wonderful aspects of our self.

BILL: So, technique number three: some form of therapeutic interaction and working with awake teachers.

ANDREW: Yes, reflection from other to self. Again, every time we see something that we once were identified with, it becomes an object that is arising within the true Self. So, how can we be that if we can see it? So, when we realize that we're not that object—because if we were, then we wouldn't be able to see it—so the more we see, the more we dis-identify, and the more our consciousness expands and we realize greater and greater levels of our true experience in our existence.

As I began to experience the soul level of my being, at first, I thought that there was a war between the soul and the ego. It was soul versus ego, which I know now is not actually the truth. It's not the way that they integrate, but at that time, my soul had all this higher wisdom informa-tion, and it had all these interesting gifts that came along with it from other experiences on my unique soul's journey through time. I started to remember experiences that were not even of this lifetime. These experi-ences were confirmed to me by healers and intuitives with whom I had not shared my personal experiences.

I had a lot of exact confirmation from many different people which helped my mind understand that I wasn't just making this stuff up or going crazy. This soul-knowing was there. I could feel deep within me that my soul had a mission or agenda. My soul had something to do on this planet, which I still feel at the core of my being that there's something that my soul is here to do. Through the journey, I eventually realized that we need to transcend this soul aspect of ourselves and realize that this is also a mistaken identity, that there's a Truth even greater to realize and to integrate, which we can point to using the common term Spirit.

However, the soul and the ego, if they're at war, or if our soul is fight-ing with the human side of ourselves, it's going to create more resistance from the human side resisting the soul's agenda, or the soul resisting the human side. We need to find a way for those two to integrate together. And the soul needs to learn to love the human as the human needs to learn to love the soul, so they can become integrated and work as a team, because they're both here existing in the Now on this planet.

BILL: What were some of the issues and challenges that the human side of you had as you became aware of your soul?

ANDREW: My experience is that my soul had a lot of information in it and a lot of, "Let's get going on this soul mission." My soul was pushing me forward really fast. And a part of my human was also wanting to move with the soul, fast. The soul has more of an unlimited resource compared to the human body; the human body is limited on this planet. The human body can't be two places at once; it has to eat, it has to sleep, it has human needs. My soul didn't have these human needs and seemed impatient. It felt like it didn't respect the human needs or maybe it just didn't fully understand them yet. I believe my human side was also not trusting my soul, so it was preventing the full integration and causing confusion in my system. It wasn't honoring that I needed this much amount of sleep. The soul was moving at speeds that my human felt like it had to try to keep up with, and it was wearing me out. So, for a while I had experiences where I was overwhelmed and tired and I was neglecting my human needs.

BILL: This is a very important point, because in classical psychiatric medicine, what you're describing—and I think this has happened for many people when they first awaken to their soul—the psychiatric community sometimes calls it a psychic break, because they're breaking out of their mold of their normal priorities. You know, normal priorities are eat, sleep, just take care of yourself. When you connect with your higher self or soul, you have this overwhelming urge to fulfill this greater destiny, and what you describe is, oh, if you don't accept the humanity of your body, you're never going to achieve what you think you're here to do. And you do have many cases that have been recorded, people literally burning themselves out because they fail to integrate. So, what were you able to do to integrate? How did you combine this new awareness of your soul's purpose without letting the soul's purpose dominate your human everyday needs?

ANDREW: Eventually, as my identity continued to widen and consciousness expanded further, there was a realization that the soul is also still a mistaken identity. It's not the true identity or the true face of our being. By transcending soul through ongoing self work, it allowed me to be able to hold both soul and human together with something else that is more of what I truly am; it can hold those two aspects in love. So, I began to learn to integrate them together.

In the integration of those two parts, first you have to see that the soul is also not the ultimate identity. There's the ultimate Spirit that is within all of us that can hold both human, or the human personality, the ego, and the soul, and all the components of the lower soul and higher soul aspects. Because the soul is pretty complex; it's not just this very basic thing; it's just like all of reality—very complex. So, by seeing it, I learned ways to integrate it, and learned to work with the human and the soul together so they can be on the same team. I'm still working on all of this today, working Now to integrate all the aspects of soul and human wholly into my being.

BILL: To recap, advice for our listener or reader. Number one, how do they become aware of their soul? And then number two, once they become aware of it, what can they do to avoid the lack of integration? Because what we've really been focusing on is the "do and the be," and combining "doing and being" in an integrated way. So, a little advice on these two topics?

ANDREW: Self-reflective practices, meditation, healing work, inner work, contemplation and journaling to see all the things that are within us that we are not, to let those things go moment by moment to realize our ultimate Truth that lovingly holds it all. Healing work, or ego work, or growing up work, anything that points us to deeper integration and true aligned realization.

Any one of those would point to releasing pathologies or parts that are stuck in these false identities that are holding energy and creating behaviors that might be causing harm to our human system and world. Basically, growing up work and waking up work combined in a way that works and honors our own system and paths, to wake up to wider identities. Then eventually, we realize soul, and once soul is realized, we understand how to work with that part of ourselves and begin to operate in the world from soul and all that comes along with that, like the essence gifts, the soul gifts, and the soul wisdom.

Eventually, through continuing the work of healing, self-reflection work, and working with people who can support us and guide us, we begin to transcend soul and integrate that aspect of us and move into higher aspects. And it may not even happen in that order. Realization can come at any time. The integration process is similar to what we do with the ego work or healing work, but it's more soul level work, and there are certain things to be done to get the soul and the human side dancing together in love. The agenda of the soul can be realized as well as the personality honored together.

BILL: It sounds like a lot of work. We need to let people know the benefits because you won't work toward something unless you realize significant benefits. What are the benefits for the ordinary person of awakening to their soul and integrating their soul with their personality?

ANDREW: To me, it's a deep commitment to awaken to my truth, and it's fun; it doesn't have to be work. It's doesn't have to be hard. If you look at it as work, it will be work. For many of us, it becomes a lot of fun. Accessing the soul levels of reality is a reality, a beautiful coming closer to home experience. There are all these amazing experiences you can have as you let go of what we believe we are from conditioning. If somebody else is operating from an integrated place in their soul level, and you're in your soul, and you interact, there's a powerful alchemy that begins to happen on the soul level that you become conscious of. And you have these amazing openings and real felt sense experiences beyond words, beyond time, that you can have with people who are also on that level and have become aware of that level.

Just like we interact in the human level, we have a soul vehicle like we have our bodies, so we can interact with our subtle bodies and there's some magical experiences that do occur. There's also what I call soul gifts, there's a lot of really cool gifts. Some of our souls have journeyed through time, through space, through dimensions. We all have different paths and individual pieces of the soul that have a lot of cool experiences and a lot of cool gifts that it's accumulated.

So, if you think of this life, as you grow up, you have a lot of skill sets you may have gained. The soul has that, and the soul has been around much, much longer than the human body and the human personality, so there's a lot of interesting gifts that start to show up that you can realize and use in this reality. There are a lot of benefits to realizing soul and also deeper well-being. Knowing the self creates this sense of joy that arises as we expand into these wider identities and letting them go as we transcend them.

BILL: Comment just briefly on some of the specifics that drive most human beings. Concern for relationships, family, career, physical health, performance.

ANDREW: I like to say there is an ROI, return on your investment, to inner work, self-inquiry and expanding your identity to soul and beyond. There's greater abundance, life magic, cool superhuman gifts, new experiences, remembrances, more pleasure in life, without the addictions and grasping, deeper connection in relationships with those you love, and much more. Even in my own relationship now, my love Felicia is opening to these higher and higher realizations. She's quite gifted, a very magical being with extraordinary abilities to guide others in this work as well. She and I have always connected on the human level, and through her own commitment and dedication to inner work and deepening into higher realizations, our relationship has evolved into both the human and the soul level.

It's such a beautiful experience that we're having, these connections, these openings. It's fun, it's deep, it's magic. Our relationship is deepening in ways that I never thought possible, never. If someone would have told me years ago this was something, I would have laughed at them and never thought there was even a reality like the one I am now experiencing. There's so much magic to be had; life becomes more of an adventure as a soul comes online and guides us. It's unlimited. Everybody has different experiences with it, and so far with most people who I've talked to that operate on the soul level, they find there's also a lot less fear than operating from just the human level. Fear begins to decrease as we realize more and more of what we are in what we can call the higher levels of reality.

BILL: My own experience, which aligns with what you're saying, is that you get to have your normal human everyday experience—everything that you know right now, if you've never explored this idea of a higher level of being—and then you get on top of that, not in opposition at all when it's integrated, this magical realm, which coexists. And it's almost as if you get to be both a human and a divine being simultaneously. As a divine being, you're aware of all the interconnections happening, all the magic that every moment of your day is somehow magically aligned by a universal love energy that you never even thought existed.

You can be comfortable with that level of being while still being the practical, everyday person, because not everyone is living at this soul level, so you still have to watch out for pickpockets and thieves and, you know, people that want to do you wrong. So, it's not this Pollyanna way of looking at the world, but there is simultaneously the magic of a perfect world of love while you also get the challenges of the imperfect world of humans. This to me is the real payoff if you are able to awaken to your true level of soul. Would you agree?

ANDREW: Absolutely. Soul is another exciting part of our being that we can choose to explore. Choose to live in along with our human life. Soul operates on a different dimension that can now easily be realized and stabilized in our everyday life experience. We all have access to this part of ourselves. Our soul has a fire in it, a burning desire to be born into the body fully to live a fully awakened life of magic and realizations. When soul and human are working together in love, we are living in unlimited potentiality.

CHAPTER ELEVEN

AWAKE IN SPIRIT

BILL: Different people use the word spirit in different ways. For you, Andrew, what do you mean when you use the word spirit?

ANDREW: For me, the word Spirit, is one of many words I use as a pointer to something that is so big, so infinite, trying to fully describe it wouldn't make much sense. Trying to encapsulate or describe what someone might call God or the All or the Infinite in words is impossible. Anything that can be said about Spirit is not the entire truth of it. We have our human experience, and from what I've experienced through my journey this far, we have all these different parts that seem to be fragmented within our human experience, and with right aligned action and intention we can expand our consciousness to an expanded pure awareness and integrate those parts into a healthy human who's operating from a deep source of inner well-being that is always here, accessible to us all.

As we stabilize and evolve through right action, our identity shifts, we can live from a deeper and wider level of our being, like soul or subtle level, which has different parts as well. As we choose to consciously evolve, our identity transcends personality as our center, to rest as soul with a personality still available to interact with the world and then eventually beyond soul. When we operate in our day to day from our soul, our inner well-being deepens, everyday fears lessen, and we have access to soul wisdom and gifts that we have cultivated through our soul's journey. As we expand even further from soul and beyond, suffering and fear continues to diminish and we can eventually integrate all the way through and realize the Awake pure nature of our being. This Awake Awareness is always ever present and each one of us can fully realize it as our absolute, true, pure nature. Then we can orient our life to a level of being that is truly free and more extraordinary than our everyday consciousness. With right action and direction we can wake up to our true nature, stabilizing this ever present, all knowing awake state into our everyday lives, beyond just sitting on a meditation cushion. We can realize that which is clear, present, pure, beyond conditioning, everywhere, nowhere, permeates everything, is everything, has always been, and will always be. Everything comes from this stable ground and will return to this. It's what some have pointed to using the terms as mind of God or Spirit or that which is Awake. The infinite. All form is made of this.

BILL: In the last chapter, we differentiated between soul and spirit. Spirit is inclusive of human personality, soul personality, and everything else. Is that correct? Or how are you defining, because when you just spoke, you were looking at spirit almost the way the Tao is described as everything and nothing.

ANDREW: Some point to Spirit as everything, some point to Spirit as nothing. Nothing is the all things are "empty" view. Like a Buddhist view. This is just language being used as pointers to certain qualities of Spirit for a realization of Spirit to occur. There's actually no way to truly describe it from everyday mind. These are just different pathways to point to Spirit. Everything view or the nothing view. Anything that can be said about Spirit is not it, words cannot describe the totality of it. Words can only point to it.

With my experience that I had with Raina, which we've discussed earlier in the book, something occurred where I blasted out, and I connected to what felt like everything in this universe and beyond. A fully interconnected, pure state of consciousness. That was an experience I had within this body, within this human experience, where I transcended this body beyond space and time. It felt like I exploded, and then it's almost like the thing I called me disappeared and there was something else there that at the core felt like it was just pure, Awake knowing, with infinitely deep love present, and I might have tasted a fraction of a fraction of a fraction of the love that was there.

And to describe this is, to me, very complicated because it feels, to me, a sacred experience that my words seem to just water down. It feels very ancient, timeless actually, beyond space, there's a presence that has always been there outside of birth and death. Now, since my experience with Raina, I've glimpsed deeper depths of what I call Spirit through my healing journey and through sitting in reflecting awareness practices I've cultivated, but I don't feel like I could truly do it justice using words to actually define what Spirit is.

BILL: When you disappeared, it wasn't just your personality that disappeared, your soul also?

ANDREW: It felt like all identification with personality, identification with soul, disappeared. It felt like all of what I thought was me shattered, then dissolved, in a positive way.

BILL: Each individual has a finite soul, and they have a finite human experience. Spirit is infinite. Is that correct?

ANDREW: Within my human experience, I have these experiences of impermanence, where things are constantly changing and shifting, and with soul and personality, these things are an evolving process, ever shifting, non-static. But there was an aspect of that experience that was absolutely eternal, beyond time, outside of time and space. And it feels like there's now a resting somewhere into that within my own experience, where I am now always feeling connected to that stable source, or can shift into that most of the day.

I feel deeply connected to it in sessions with my clients, or working with others, being of service. It feels like it's the source of what deeply moves me and through me. It's the source of what animates life or animates this reality, but it's an eternal aspect that everything has come from, everything will return to. Even saying that doesn't feel quite correct, because nothing actually goes through it, nothing actually leaves it. It is always there. It is always. Just is always.

BILL: Many people have used the expression, "We're not human beings having a spiritual experience, we're spiritual beings having a human experience." You're using spirit in a different way from that, because in that sentence, it seems that they're talking about a spiritual being as a soul being. So, differentiate, because we're sort of getting near, but it is very similar. We talked about the Tao. The Tao that can be described isn't the Tao. And to some extent, it almost seems as if you're saying the same thing about spirit. The spirit that can be defined isn't the spirit, it has to be experienced. You've had, as you say, just a little drop of the experience, if you think of it as an ocean. So, this is a difficult concept to convey, and of course, at the end of conveying it, we want to also provide the listeners and the readers with why this is relevant to their lives, because if you've never experienced this realm, why does it matter?

ANDREW: I think what you're pointing to, not being able to describe it, like what they say in the Tao, is how it feels. It feels very, very true to me. I had that experience, and then I read about Lao Tzu and the Tao. It had a lot of resonance to my experience. You cannot explain this, how can anyone explain infinity? It can't be explained. Now why does it matter? When I started the journey, I began from the perspective of not consciously looking for Spirit, not for God, or for this Infinite Pure Presence. I was interested in truly knowing myself, with an intention for health and well-being.

I was hoping to feel better. I was hoping to get answers to why my life felt like disconnection and suffering. Through my journey, I opened up to this amazing adventure that still continues to unfold. Something very intelligent, a wisdom that began to lead me on this journey. When I became aware of my internal experience, there was an intelligence that led me through a really beautiful process, led me to this experience where I reconnected back to what we're calling Spirit. It taught me, took great care of me on this path when I decided to truly know myself.

Why that matters is because I didn't know that I was missing a connection with something that is Truth within me. I felt there was a hole inside me that I didn't even know was needing to be filled, and it was really deep and painful. When I reconnected back to Spirit, that hole has now been mended. It feels that I'm no longer stuck in unnecessary suffering. I feel truly fulfilled. I still experience the whole range of emotions, with many ups and downs in my human life. But I feel like I'm no longer fixated or lost searching for something. I get to be fully present with all my experiences and with who I'm with. Through this discovery of Spirit, not intentionally finding it, I am now operating more from an

Awake Alignment with my soul energy activated, connected through to my human parts, and with others in the world. I feel deeply fulfilled and amazing because of that connection.

BILL: Let's reflect without naming any names on your client base. Your clients represent normal human beings. They may be more successful than most and more motivated to discover than most, but one of the observations I've made is that almost every human being at one point or another in their life feels something's missing. Either they're struggling to get something and they're not getting it, or they actually obtain what they were struggling to get and they are deflated because it's never as life altering as they thought it might be.

It occurs to me when you start talking about your own experience, and why the concept of spirit, just the concept of spirit in the way that you're defining it, could be important to any one is if, at some point in your life, you are experiencing either the struggle to obtain, or obtaining and then feeling deflated, knowing that there's a totally different realm that is coexisting with your preprogrammed realm, that might actually be what you are truly seeking and bring you to a place where you're no longer seeking.

ANDREW: I find this to be true, I found out that this is a very common story throughout the history of personal development and spirituality. We hear when people find their idea of success, they still feel very unfulfilled. There's something to be said about having success. I think it's okay to have success and to enjoy life. But when you enjoy from a connection to this true inner being, this Spirit that is flowing through all of us, there's something really special about every moment that we experience. It feels deeply fulfilling.

Many of my clients work on different levels of reality, from human development, belief systems, to energetics, to the soul level, to essence gifts. I'm not here to bring anybody to Spirit. That's not something that I offer. But I have pointers that are pointing to something, and there are times where I'm with clients and this sacred magic has occurred, where my clients have dropped into this pure knowing Awake Awareness or this Spirit that is always ever present, and that experience is beyond words, it is profound for me and who I'm with to be in that union together and to experience that. I have witnessed bright, energetic, translucent energy coming off them, they look vibrant, their faces are in utter shock, filled with love and joy.

BILL: One of the things that most human beings are seeking is inner peace. Comment how becoming aware of Spirit can bring someone to inner peace.

ANDREW: Prior to my experience of reconnecting back to what we're calling Spirit here, I felt chaos. I felt unease, I felt anxiety always, I felt separate and alone. In addition, there was resistance to all life, and I was disconnected from myself, from my emotions. I wasn't peaceful. I may have looked peaceful on the outside; might have looked stoic or peaceful, but I don't feel I ever was. Ever since this experience, there's always in the background this depth of peace that seems to exist, no matter how chaotic things are in my everyday life. I feel connected to all things.

When anxiety arises, there's a center of peace; when there's happiness or joy, there's peace. It's arising from this deep well of well-being that I found within myself, as I reconnected to this pure state that is always there, has always been there. And that continues to deepen as I continue my journey and continue to act from my Awake Alignment. It's like in the past, maybe I was lost in the surrounding storms of a hurricane, but now I'm resting as the eye of the hurricane and everything's floating around me without any real impact. In that eye is the Absolute Presence, peace. It looks empty, but it's not empty; it's full of love, full of infinite potential and it permeates everything, and I'm just resting as the open clear space as the eye, or an aspect of me is resting in that eye, while chaos is all around me. If a life storm comes to pull me out for a ride, I do my inner work to shift or I am able to just shift back as the eye letting the storm pass.

BILL: So Spirit seems to be a state of being, but explain how Spirit can also influence the doing.

ANDREW: Being, like all there is, arises from Spirit. All states are not separate from Spirit. Within that being, when we're fully present with ourselves, with our being, with our Awake Alignment, energy and Spirit creator energy begins to move us to right action. Spirit brings us into alignment with what we're here to do, with connection with others. Things work themselves out when we're aligned to Spirit. I find there's power. Spirit fire that moves and animates all life.

Eckhart Tolle actually has said spiritual power moves through what we do when we are in Presence acting from being. I feel he's pointing to the power of being, operating in the world from Awake Alignment with Presence in all that we do in the Now, or what the Tao points to as effortless action with no small self—the Way, where when we're resting in being without a small self, the awake energy of this reality, of this universe, begins to move us and begins to guide us and we dance with that energy of creation. Fully awake with awake energy. Life becomes an unfolding adventure that most of us can't even imagine. Instead of trying to manifest reality or create reality, because along this path you can learn to do that, if you even let that go, amazing things will start to unfold that you never could have expected. A relationship might show up, you never thought possible. Magic can show up in this reality beyond what most people could imagine. More and more of my clients are opening up to that, they're seeing that, they are having these experiences. It's becoming more integrated in their everyday life. To me, there's nothing more fulfilling than being aligned with Spirit. To me, that's all there is.

BILL: Let's explore the manifestation dance. If you rely solely on Spirit, where's the juice? Because Spirit is complete and empty and full. Spirit in and of itself. It's not like when you have your soul's mission and you're saying, "Ah, I've got to do this. It's just, "Ah, isn't everything perfect." So there needs to be a dance between isn't everything perfect, which it is, and whether you want to go to the level of the human personality or the soul mission. But it seems to me that it's this intersection of the two where the doing can happen. And the difference between the doing that's either from the personality or just the soul, as opposed to the doing that's informed by Spirit [is that] the doing when it's informed by Spirit is not only effortless, it's unfolding in the course of spirit events, which is timeless.

So, when we look at other sages who have talked about manifestation, such as Napoleon Hill and others, they focus on you have to have a thought, you have to access—they don't use the word spirit—but, whether we're calling it the zero point or we're calling it Universal Mind, they are aware that you need to access something that's universal. But then their focus is, you need to really focus and have desire. So, how do you respond to this level of dance? How does one integrate letting everything go, the being, and maybe really wanting something, which is more the doing? ANDREW: If we remain only resting in Spirit or as a pure Awake Awareness avoiding life then this could be a spiritual bypass. This has been known to happen. Awake Awareness is a pure mind of Spirit state that all humans can realize. It is always present right in front of us. When we realize there's a pure Awake state of mind, we can rest as it and then from there learn to allow life energy to simultaneously begin to move us and through us, integrating Awake Awareness all the way through our system. Healing is a great tool to use to awaken to all levels of our being, allowing us to take enlightened, awake, compassionate action in our world. We can have our life experiences while no longer getting lost in them. There's different, confused, false parts of ourselves that could be in control of our system that might be trying to separate ourselves from living fully awake. I feel we need a high level of commitment and dedication to being in alignment.

With right doing we can get out of our own way allowing this Awake all knowing intelligence that knows how to take right action in the world to guide our life. An example of this intelligence I use, if somehow I cut myself, it's going to heal itself; there's an always present intelligence that knows to take over and heal my body. Now, if the cut is really deep, I might need to assist that by listening to this intelligence then taking right action and getting stitches. So, there's a right doing that assists the natural wisdom to do the work that it does. I think that's something we can do and we can extrapolate that to all areas of life. If my life has a small cut in it, let's say, the intelligence, if I allow it through right aligned action, will work itself out and things will resolve themselves, and situations will resolve themselves. Effortless mindfulness, inner healing work, attachment repair, and self reflection practices are some examples of right doing. Those examples of right practices are like the stitches to assist the healing of deep inner wounds and trauma.

If the cut is really deep, or magnified—you know, chop off a finger— then I might need to do a little surgery, go to the Western medicine to fix this, to let the intelligence do its work. My life was kind of messy, like a chopped off finger, and I needed to find a way to get the natural intelligence back online and allow the wisdom to guide me, and through self-reflecting practices, through alignment work, through right doing with a true intention to know myself and heal, I began that dance with the intelligence, and it woke me up, and I woke up to it.

The dance still happens and guides me. Sometimes I go off course, but I come back into Awake Alignment through right action and it then guides me again. There's also ways you can play with reality when you're centered in Presence. You can experiment with reality in profound ways while being centered in Presence. Reality actually energetically responds to Presence. You can play with some really interesting things between these energetics that exist in people and forms using the power of Awake Awareness. Relating with others from these higher levels, from soul and essence, can be wild and full of wisdom and magic. So, you can play with the "doing," but it's always resting in the "Being" when you want Intelligence or Spirit to be there to guide in the way that I'm describing through aligned action.

BILL: Two concepts jump out at me: awareness and alignment. In the dance of manifestation, awareness and alignment seem fundamental. If you were completely unaware that you even have a cut, Spirit may want to assist in repair, but you might bleed out if it's a deep enough cut. On a metaphorical level, I think many human beings are walking around with very deep cuts and they're not even aware. In many cases, they're also not in alignment with Spirit. This is a fundamental cause of suffering.

On the other extreme, there's been reports of Buddhist monks who were murdered during the Vietnam War, and they were in so much alignment, that even though they saw that they had nothing they could do to avoid being murdered, they were at peace, because they were already gone to some extent. They were accepting that the All That Is was taking them on this journey, and it was not up to them to escape it. They didn't have fear, they didn't have sorrow; they just had accep-tance. They were reported to be smiling at those who were killing them, which defies our normal thought process of how one of us might react if someone was about to shoot us. What are some of the techniques you've used with clients to remain aware and aligned with Spirit? ANDREW: Presence and being fully with what is, lovingly embracing all that arises and learning to cultivate acceptance from the level of pure open hearted awareness for all of the lost parts of self, and learning to stay and be with what's happening inside ourselves no matter how exciting, how joyful, or how painful and how scary it is. Teaching them about their unique energetic constitutions to find their doorways to open easily into open hearted Awake Alignment. Living each moment in the Now from a place of presence, being with all that is arising. From there, the awake energy of Spirit takes over. There's something that begins to happen, where even in my own sessions with clients, I had to learn to drop all expectations by being with the expectations when they arise, then they drop away, and when I get out of my own way, I'm being led in the sessions through this awake intelligent energy that is very wise, and very deep, that knows directly and it leads me while I'm in that place of Presence.

How I actually translate that in everyday life is when I want to work on my own alignment, I have to drop deeply into expansive presence and not lie to myself at all. Being really radically truthful to what is, to what's arising in my emotional body experience within the physical body, the mental body, being with it all from an open hearted awareness no matter how uncomfortable. And I had to learn that through cultivating certain skill sets and increasing my emotional intelligence, deepening self-reflective practices, working with others through mentorships and healing work. What I'm pointing to here is learning to be radically truthful with yourself, learning to—no matter how uncomfortable it is—not lying anymore to what's there within our experience, to be fully present with what is. And through the wisdom of truth and the wisdom of Awake Alignment, that wisdom starts to wake up within you and within others around you, and it starts to guide you through life. So, that's one of the biggest components of this—no longer lying to yourself. Radical truth and radical acceptance.

BILL: Provide a background on how we know what is true for ourselves, because, as we discussed earlier in this book, most of us come in with parents who mean well and who have been programmed and who are passing along this programming, much of which is, in fact, not based on truth at all. How does one differentiate between, quote, "programmed false truth" and "true truth?"

ANDREW: There was a point in my journey that we spoke about in an earlier chapter where I began the inward turn, and then I eventually had that realization that I've been lying to myself all this time, and I had to take full responsibility in order to take back my power over living in victim consciousness. It's not that I forced truth upon myself; I had a realization that I was lying. There is a process that unfolds as we go in, with courage, with love, and care for ourselves and for our experience, and we stop lying to ourselves, because if you try to "do" truth, that's not really it; it has to unfold naturally, and it's a process. No one can give you your truth.

There are ways to speed it up. Like learning to locate our local awareness that is bound in everyday confusion or when it's lost in stuck parts, then uncoupling it to then rest in our truth to then come back to lovingly release those parts of self that are stuck in mistaken identities. There's different techniques that can be done with aligned guidance for our unique systems that can support us in getting out of our own way. Let me give an example. When I came here, a part of me was nervous about this chapter. It's like, I'm about to speak about this huge topic of Spirit. Who am I to speak about the Infinite, you know? There was fear arising in the background with this inner talk. And I'm sitting here and listening to myself speak, in this moment, with everybody in this room, there is a small, young part of me still doubting what I'm saying. There's a small part that is in fear within me. There's a part of me that doesn't know if it's going to be received very well. And I'm speaking radical truth right now from that part within me. This part needs my attention. My loving kindness with absolute agenda-less radical acceptance for it to feel safe to allow me to speak from my highest truth in this moment, or it could hijack my system, blocking the flow of this chapter. I've learned to tend to my confused parts moment by moment so they don't take over of my experience. I can come back to them later to integrate them at a more appropriate time.

BILL: Well, the fear part is Andrew the human being.

ANDREW: Part of my system. Yes. A small part of Andrew the human being, yes.

BILL: Is any of Andrew the soul experiencing fear? Is it just the human?

ANDREW: As I feel into it, I can feel the depths of the emotional body, the soul, the mental body. You're actually pointing to something I find to be really profound. In the past, you might have asked me this question, I would have had no idea how to answer. I can feel my soul is really excited to talk about this topic. I feel the soul's agenda here, to speak about this journey. It's exciting, we're talking about Spirit, sharing this amazing experience, this amazing journey we've been on. The personality parts that exist, parts that make up the idea of Andrew, the old conditioned personality, there's still structures and small false identities in there, again, who are questioning and have been asking, "Who am I to speak about this?" "What will people think of me?"

These parts rise and fall and I just witness them in real time from a spacious, loving awareness with this now strong reflective local awareness skill in the moment and not go on the ride with them. They dissolve back from where they came into a warm energy. In this moment, I can also feel there's loving, awake energy flowing through my body where I can feel the parts of my heart that are wide open. I can feel loving, awake energy flowing down through my legs right now, and on another level of my being, I can feel emotional energy moving through me of excitement, nervousness. Awake energy all around my body in this room.

All this stuff is rising and falling in each moment. Moment by moment, I'm able to deeply feel many levels of this in my being and all around me. It took deep dedication to cultivate these skill sets to get to where I am now with my awareness to know what is my truth and what is not. This allows me to speak from my truth and to hold the other small parts that are living in separation in a loving awareness, or at least without identifying with them so that they can relax while this book is flowing through.

BILL: What I'm observing, which I think is going to be of great help to readers and listeners is, in your case, in this moment, we are differentiating between the false truth of your programming; the Andrew that has been told there's no way you're possibly intelligent enough or wise enough to talk about something as deep as Spirit. And that's actually a false truth. And it's that false truth that is who you are, that has created the fear, because your soul level and beyond your soul, just from Spirit, I mean, there's no question that this is a high level truth; there's no ambiguity. It may be difficult to, quote, "prove or disprove," but it's certainly without programming. It's authentic. I think this is a good illustration for beginning the process of separating our preconditioned, quote, "false truth" from authentic truth.

As you've said in other chapters, it's also the protector. It's important to acknowledge that that "false truth" has served a purpose and has not been evil. It's been effective. In most cases, you could call them defense mechanisms that got you through very difficult situations. If you want to rise to the next level of being, you have to let go. And it's sort of like, "when I was a child, I played with childish things," and now I'm an adult, and I'm ready. That's the greeting, and to some extent challenge, we're offering to readers. There's no necessity. There's a lot of nice things about staying a child your whole life. If that's your choice, you're not condemned for it. But be aware that it's a choice, and that there will be some negative fallout, probably, if you make that choice.

ANDREW: Absolutely. I feel that to be true. One of the things that I felt was important when I started to do this work is that I absolutely had a clear intention to discover myself. I feel, to have a clear intention to reconnect back, if you feel guided to reconnect back to Spirit or back to Self, with that pure intention, you will be guided. That reality will be your reality. There's something to that. If it's a clear commitment within ourselves to discover what truth is, and discover our truth, there's a wisdom that truly guides us in our own unique way. A wisdom that loves us all equally without any conditions that is waiting for us to return home. Something wakes up in this universe, wakes up to that intention, it feels like it wakes something up in the universe that begins to take over, takes control in a way that is loving, caring, and wants you to find that truth. A natural, loving wisdom intelligence that is accessible to us all when pure intention is there.

BILL: The three As: Alignment, Awareness, and Action. If you're able to incorporate all three, I think that you're uniquely evolved to a state where you can access not just everyday reality, but higher levels of reality which coexist. This is sometimes a difficult concept for someone who's not had an experience as you've had, or as I've had with my near-death experience. But there are different realities coexisting on this planet. Insofar as you can shapeshift to some extent, back and forth between these realities, you can thrive in them all.

This is something that those who have been traditionally trained to just, "Well, I can't touch and feel it, so it doesn't exist," may say, "No... I think these guys are full of hot air." That's fine, too. But you might also say, "Well, even if they're full of hot air, let's just explore it a little bit." And when you're ready to explore it, I think there's been some great insights provided in this book—or audio, if you're listening. We can make a difference. People are ready to start living on a higher level with greater complexity that is, ironically, also a way to simplify your life. It makes things a lot simpler, too. Do you have any other final comments on the topic of Spirit?

ANDREW: One thing that really stands out when I feel into this, or feel the presence of Spirit, is that there's a depth of embrace and care that is always there. The deeper I connect with it, the more that that care deepens within myself, to others, and to myself. I feel that there's just something to the alignment. That Awake Awareness, alignment, and action, the three As. I feel like that is well said. I'd like to add that all three of those qualities should be embraced with love and compassion.

BILL: Well, it's very interesting, as you were saying that, I immediately had the experience of my near death, in which the only thing that really dominated was this sense of love. Love is the foundation of it all. I think that for you to bring love back to this otherwise esoteric discussion is very valuable, because I think everyone has had an experience of love, and that it is a way of starting the individual journey. Ultimately, everyone wants to experience love on as many levels and in as many ways as possible. We can love a plant. We love pets. We love people. There is the love of art, music; but it's even more profound than that. You can have the love of a chair, you can have the love of your hair, of anything. So, I think that's very well focused to say that the firmament is really the firmament of love.

ANDREW: I also want to ask a question about your near-death experience when you were hovering above—because I think we talked about this—you were hovering above your body. And from what you described, that was what was there. But you could see yourself, right? You could recognize your body, yes?

BILL: Well, the body, I didn't recognize it as my body. Frankly, I still don't really identify. I go back and forth. When I'm eating, and when I'm doing

sports, this is my body. But there's also a level of my being at this point where it's just a body; it's not really *my* body. It's kind of on loan to me.
ANDREW: For sure. So, that's that impermanence of the body. You know that you're not your body, is what I'm hearing. And there's something more true to your being. But when you share the story, you mention you could see the body that you were once embodying.
BILL: Right, but that's the same way I could see a chair or a table.
ANDREW: And how long were you dead for?
BILL: I don't really know. It could have been two minutes, it could have been less, just seconds. But it doesn't really matter, because when you're in that state, time ceases to exist altogether. So, whether it was two seconds, two minutes—I know it wasn't much longer than that, or I wouldn't have been able to get back to the body. I would have been long gone. But it wasn't long enough for the body to cease complete functioning.
ANDREW: What I hear, though, is in your experience with love being there, there's also something really cool that I would like to point to, is that, beyond the brain you have a direct knowing that that was your body, that love was there. There was a recognition. There's something that knows not only from a level of human mind, of our own brain or human intelligence. In that Awake Awareness, in that love, there's an intelligence that knows beyond everyday mind. I think with your description of how you describe your near-death experience, you were outside your body with an absolute knowing. It shows us not only is there love, but there's an intelligence in that love that has direct recognition of experience.
BILL: There definitely is awareness, an intelligent awareness. You can call it intelligence. There was awareness, there was alignment, and then in my particular case, and this is the human element I really do see, the action takes place at the human level. It was the action I took of willing the being that I am back into the body. If you recall the story, the love was really more about the love for the doctor—not wanting the doctor to have killed someone inadvertently. And so, there was compassion. But the love that I experienced, that was a minor afterthought, actually.

The real love was the experience of complete bliss. Just complete bliss without a care in the world, literally. I wasn't in the world. And it was a feeling that gets to your initial comments from this chapter about how can you describe something that's indescribable? How can you use words? It can't be done. And we made our entire film, *Tapping the Source*, from the premise that how do we explain that the most blissful moment as a human being—and I've had a very blissful life; all these wonderful things have happened—came when I wasn't even, quote/unquote, "alive?" What is this about? It really makes you stop and think. There's a lot of food for thought here that allows readers and listeners to go forth and enjoy their own unique experiences of being part of this incredible spirit universe.

ANDREW: Thank you for sharing your story Bill. As we peer out into the vastness of space or deep down into the depth of the quantum in awe, we continue to see how little we know. As we open ourselves back up to Spirit by opening back up to trusting that reality is a part of us and is working for us when we are working with it, then we will find greater and greater ease, adventure, abundance and the love that was always there waiting for us all.

CHAPTER TWELVE

LIVING, LOVING, LEARNING, STILL IN AWE

BILL: Andrew is now living in awe of the human experience, and he's in awe of his own journey. He's not at the end of his journey by any means. In fact, I think it would be best to say he's really only at the beginning, but he's at a beginning that's coming from a place of integration, which is what we've been talking about, and integration allows one to still have the complete awe of the human experience and the spiritual experience, because it's not just being a human anymore.

Other writers who I represent, such as Barbara Marx Hubbard and Neil Donald Walsch, have talked about "we are spiritual beings having a human experience." And that is true. At this time on this planet, for the first time it's possible to have spiritual experiences at the level of Spirit that goes beyond everyday human experience. Not just for Andrew (Andrew is really a representative at this time for the challenge as well as the possibility of human evolution).

Andrew is no more special than you or I. One might even say he was less than special; he was a less than zero to some. He didn't have the basic elements, if you've read earlier chapters in this book, for having a, quote, "successful life." And then he had a near-death experience in which he had to overcome physical and mental and emotional challenges that were even greater than those that he had already inherited. From that point of view, Andrew is a good symbol for everyone of what can happen once you integrate. Andrew has now spent many years, you've heard it in this book, on the integration, the self-reflection, all the practices that he's done, and what he's been able to do with his clients to lead them on this path. Andrew, what do you see as your mission and your life's purpose and how that directly interacts with the higher destiny of our planet?

ANDREW: I love the word awe. It's absolutely how I feel. Most of my day, I walk around feeling awe with life. That continues to deepen. Life continues to give me magic curveballs that I've never expected in ways that are amazing. I think the adventure that I'm on now is more stable than what it once was, and the magic continues to deepen. The intimacy with myself and others continues to deepen. Truth flows out of me in ways that I'm even stunned to hear coming through me, coming out of me. I feel like I'm learning every day from myself. I feel like my clients are some of my greatest teachers. My relationship is one of my biggest teachers.

Sitting here doing this book with Bill, Gayle, Felicia in these sessions, I've learned so much. I've deeply enjoyed it. I didn't know I was going to be doing a book with Bill Gladstone. I had no idea I'd be sitting here doing this. I said to Felicia recently, "Wow, this is amazing." I get to share a book about my journey at this amazing place in Cardiff by the Sea with the sun setting in the background, sky lit up, its brilliant warm colors cascading over the ocean, in this amazing house, and all the while having this incredible experience full of energy and love. I'm absolutely in awe and blessed that I'm having these experiences now in my life, and it's fun.

So, life continues to deepen, to open in ways that are full of fun, and adventures keep unfolding. I still have my emotional experiences. I still have some stress. I was trying to get here on time, trying to get the other chapters printed for the book today, and I had my little bit of stress that came up, "Got to get it ready, have it prepared, don't be late." That kind of minor anxiety still exists, but it's no longer impacting me in ways that throw me for a loop and derail me from life.

I've continued to deepen my alignment, am able to quickly bounce back from [being overwhelmed], and while in Awake Alignment, magic continues to be the overall theme of my life. I mean that in a way that it's available to everybody, and I see that in everybody. I see the unlimited potential of everybody who walks through my door, who works with me, who stands in front of me. I see the depths of what we have in us and what's possible, and I see that ongoing. I will continue to deepen my own connection to myself, to my being, to my well of internal well-being, so I can be a carrier of that wisdom, so I can embody that wisdom, so I can transmit that wisdom in whatever way, whatever capacity that looks like. That is a deep commitment that I have to myself and to all beings.

I have a deep care that is not coming from a vow or a commitment of the mind; it arises naturally from the core of my heart, from a loving aspect of myself that feels that we all have the potential to do so much on this planet. Each individual has a potential in them that is waiting to be unlocked. If I can offer an insight or a word of wisdom or some feedback or a healing session or a coaching session, or group work session—whatever that looks like to support bringing that potential through—that's where I'm going to stand and continue to align while living my human experience in magic and awe, while also deepening my own adventure in this life.

BILL: One of the concepts that I really like is the concept of magic. Not so much the magic that is trickery, because there is a lot of trickery, and not so much the magic that is flashy like, "Oh, how did the tiger get out of the cage or in the cage." But the idea of magic more in the sense of the magic of the universe. The magic that happens, and then you do turn around, you say, "That was awesome, it was just awesome." I think that your journey is about awesomeness. I think it's about living an awesome life. So, explain what living an awesome life means for you.

ANDREW: That's a great question. Authentic, deep connection with others and with energy is part of an awesome life for me. I think of the concept of energy when I hear this. Energy to me is like a language. I see it, I speak it, the universe speaks it. We call it vibration, energy, sound waves. I feel below what we call matter, below the surface of reality, there is this magic. It's like a clay. There's a substance that can become any experience, that can create states, that can create pleasure, create joy, create pain, be formed into parts, or protectors. It's this infinite potential.

When you learn to speak that language of energy and you learn the fundamental aspects of this universe and how to communicate with it, magic is just there waiting to be connected to. Magic seems to be a watered-down word for what is possible and what is the potential that lies within this clay, this pure potentiality of energy, this infinite source that we've been taught to fight over on the planet. Energy is one of the absolute fundamental building blocks of this universe, and when you learn to speak energy, and you swim in energy, and you're enjoying energy, magic is bound to show up. It points me to that very topic, this infinite clay that we can play in and be with and enjoy altogether. For me, living an awesome life is knowing that this potential for infinite possibility is a reality, and it leads to an awe-some life. Anything becomes possible, and it becomes a reality. We are creators only from this true realization.

BILL: It makes me think of our grandchildren. We were just walking on the beach the other day. You have all these little kids running around building sandcastles. The water is going to knock them all down, but it doesn't matter because they're all in the moment and they're all just totally amazed at the whole scenario. The fact they can build the sandcastle. The fact that the water is going to take it away, and the fact that they can build walls and delay the water. It's all just play.

I think at the highest level, that's all humanity has, is play. All we have is play. Why are we here? What do we represent? You can get all serious and historical, and we're here like *Game of Thrones* to save the people from evil. There's a level where all that can be true, but fundamentally, it's not really about good and evil at all. It's just about the play. We're here as part of Spirit, and Spirit is playful. Spirit is just enjoying the ride. It doesn't have a destination because it's already there.

I think that part of what you've been able to do with your clients and with yourself by letting go of all of your preconceived conditioning, you just sort of, "Let's see where this journey is going to take me, let's see what's next." So, when I ask you what is an awesome life, it's interesting, most people would have said things like, "Well I want to be rich and I want to have a big house and all the cars, and then I want to have children and grandchildren, and I want to have a legacy, and I want to make the world a better place," and all these things that one could realistically hope for. You may hope for them as well as part of an awesome life, but you didn't mention any of those things. You mentioned energy. In that way, I think you've hit on something that's much more universal, because everything else is just an end product of energy.

ANDREW: Totally. I absolutely agree. I love how you're speaking of the children at play in the sand, and one of the things that I imagine when I hear you say this is that they are playing together, and they're not by themselves, and to be honest there's probably a little bit of a selfish aspect to this work. I do this work in part because I want people to play with in the infinite possibilities. I want others to join me in alignment because it's fun, and there's unbelievable experiences that happen. I also care deeply about the well-being of this world and humanity.

I tell everybody I work with, "Don't believe me, you don't need to believe anything I'm saying. Have your own experience and I'll be your guide in any way I can, and I'll do the best that I can." I'm committed to that. But I don't want anybody just to blindly believe the words I'm saying because this experience that I have had is not special in the way that it's just for me. Others are having it; other people are waking up to these experiences. I want to play with more people in this reality in a way that is not just focused on accumulating things. Things are great. It's good to have a house and security and safety and money and abundance, and I think this is a part of life, but my focus is something deeper because that feels more aligned. And it's so good, it's so enjoyable to be in that with others. That's why I focus on that, because I think playing with others in this experience is what we are here to do. This play can be expressed in an infinite number of ways.

BILL: It's even more profound than that. If you go back to Eckhart Tolle's *The Power of Now*, there's a page in which he says, if you're feeling what I'm describing, please share this book with others because it is the collective energy of others waking up to this higher state of awareness that gives this state of awareness a better chance of being the primary state for humanity. And so, it really is, as you go on your individual journey, an opportunity to help others, because it really is a matter of the more people that have these higher states of awareness, alignment matching, the better the chances are that humanity as a whole—whether half a billion people in some remote part of the world have no idea what we're talking about— will still benefit, because it is all about vibration.

When I was referring to these multiple realities co-existing, it's really higher states of vibration co-existing. My experience is the higher the vibration, the more effortless the manifestation, and the greater the experience of love. You can experience love and it's wonderful, you know, with a woman, with your children, with your grandchildren, and it's hard for me to ask anyone to take it on faith, but my own experience was, all those levels of love is not even on the scale of one to ten in terms of the experience of love when you are in the infinite state of Spirit. And that this is available. We can all move closer and closer to that state without having to drop the body, without having to go through rigorous training.

I've never been a big fan of, "You gotta go on these diets," and "You gotta go into isolation." People go to [such an] extreme that they bury themselves for thirty days in the dirt—none of that is really necessary. You can get there in very simple ways. One of the reasons I've been so open with Andrew and making available the time to co-create this book with him is he hasn't really done anything extraordinary. The only thing extraordinary was he got knocked in the head. But other than that, the way he's gotten himself to where he is, away from lost and confused, just to a healthy state of awe, is by observing, healing, becoming still, and doing very contemplative work.

It's not hard work. Once you start, it's almost—for me, I would say it's equivalent to doing a crossword puzzle where it's interesting, yes, sometimes you get stuck, but it's not really that hard, and it's amusing. That's why we do the puzzles. So, in Andrew's case, his puzzle was, "How do I get from this state of complete chaos to a state where I'm not so nervous and confused?" That was the puzzle that he was attempting to solve, and he solved it. He is not dazed. He is not confused. He is in awe. He's not really sure what's going to happen in the next ten minutes in his life, but he's okay with that. I think from that perspective, Andrew is both a teacher and a model for what hopefully is the new evolving human being.

ANDREW: My primary advice is just go easy on yourself and others. Life is an interesting journey, and everybody has their own unique experience, their own unique experience of what we call Spirit or religion or whatever way they are approaching it. I think we need to honor all ways and just know that there is a truth at some level in all those ways. If we come from that, at the very least, if we can just shift into honoring and going easy on ourselves and others, a lot can happen just from that alone. Old constructs begin to fall away. I always find that going easy on ourselves and each other is probably always a good word of advice for anyone. With all the current constructs that are in place, constructs that we all have agreed upon that make up this current reality, some of these can be tough to deal with. We need to go easy, have compassion while these constructs begin to shift.

CHAPTER THIRTEEN
INTO THE FLOW

BILL: As we conclude this book, we come to the realization that the principles that Andrew teaches enable people to get into alignment that allows for flow. Getting into the flow combines the best of doing with the best of being; you're doing effortlessly, and you're being completely. And this happens when you're in the flow. Other people have written about being in the flow, and it's a phenomenon that has been documented. Great athletes get into the flow; everything appears effortlessly. A tennis player or baseball player sees the ball and it's almost as if it's in slow motion.

Part of the reason getting in the flow is so productive and desirable, is it removes the separation of you as a personality from the larger life force in which you are operating, and everything that may have seemed like an obstacle becomes a resource. This is why other great thinkers—Goethe is probably the most famous—once you make up your mind to do something, the universe aligns itself to your purpose. So, Andrew, talk a little bit about what it is like for you and your clients when they're in the flow. How you can enhance opportunities to be in the flow. And once in the flow, to stay in the flow.

ANDREW: It's very common that people talk about spontaneously accessing a flow state. Over the years, I have contemplated what flow means, and what exactly is that feeling or that clear state that everyone is talking about? For me, through proper integration of Awake Alignment into our life, I feel there's many depths of flow that we can reach and stabilize for ongoing periods of life until flow ultimately becomes an easeful ongoing way of life. By expanding our awareness, through healing and with right practices we can learn to shift into flow states, eventually stabilizing it. Until flow is fully stable, we can learn to easily glimpse it daily to deepen our connection into flow to eventually live only from it. There's also different experiences of being in flow states that human beings seem to experience in our reality.

Some of us experience being in a deep kinesthetic state of flow, like an athlete when they hit a flow state leading into total union with body and a clear mind resulting in a superhuman performance that looks so effortless and easeful. Athletes like Kobe Bryant in basketball or Michael Jordan would display these flow state abilities. These beings are connected to high levels of kinesthetic body intelligence, that when in a flow state, they are so far above the rest.

As we deepen and understand our own systems, we can connect on all these different levels of intelligence—human intelligence, cognitive intelligence, different levels of mind, kinesthetic intelligence, emotional intelligence, psychic intelligence—and as we learn to access deep flow states, superhuman things seem to occur. Accessing the flow state through Presence by learning to expand our local awareness to its pure expanded awake state, then allowing awake energy to flow through us is possible when we are being totally in our truth—in the moment, we can open our doorway, being fully present in the Now—and as we develop greater access shifting into flow, we can continue to deepen experiences, eventually living in flow by orienting into right alignment and operating from truth. As we learn to map our systems and learn to understand what is preventing us from shifting into and living in flow, we can learn how to kindly work with ourselves, to deepen our access, untie the internal knots, and to be able to shift deeper and faster into flow to experience the highest performance in all areas of life.

BILL: One of the things you had mentioned was that it's not just about the individual personality, it's about your system, the human system. I would add that it even goes beyond the human system. My own experience of being in the flow I've experienced in my business life. What Gayle and I often talk about is we've created a vortex of energy, and the vortex of energy just pulls in whatever you want. Part of this is being focused and in alignment with your desires. There is a human doing, but then there's also a human detachment. It's paradoxical. There was a time when Waterside was so focused on helping technically proficient authors that it was literally magic.

Someone would walk in the door wanting a book on the subject, and within minutes, someone would call with the ability to write that book. We were in a flow that was effortless, completely effortless. However, we were also paying attention. We were also focused on the outcome, on this positive result of bringing forth opportunities for our authors to write these books about technology. We were aligned with a higher purpose that we didn't even understand at the time, which was that people really needed to learn how to use this technology.

It served a much larger purpose than just the money we would make as an agency, or the money the author would make, or the money the publisher would make; it actually, in its own way, was a great contributor to what we now have as the internet and everything else of interconnecting all of human life. One of the things that I'm interested in asking you is, in terms of systems, not just in terms of the individual, how—because you've talked before about how groups can come together in a flow—once you're established in terms of your individual well-being, the natural next step seems to be to create group well-being.

ANDREW: This is a great example of how you've created a field that allows for flow within your own everyday reality of your business. I naturally stumbled into experiencing this as I deepened integration of my entire system of being through the integration of my human parts and the different parts of my soul. I've noticed through holding stabilized, right Awake Alignment, which you called focus, a field of energy emerged in my life and body that allowed for easeful flow to naturally arise in my everyday life that continues to sustain for longer and longer periods of time.

It was like magic where things that were hard in the past began to effortlessly come easy, where perfectly timed opportunities would magically show up through this flow. Naturally and organically, my business has aligned with my life, and I am living my purpose on the planet with joy and much less fear. The perfect clients have always shown up without any effort. As I showed up each day of my life authentically committed to being of service deep within my core alignment, everything I needed effortlessly came to me. I did not have to market at all to grow my successful practice, and still don't to this day.

I teach many of my clients who are successful entrepreneurs, coaches, and healers, that found their success through the output of tremendous energy and hard work, how to use less energy and bring in more effortless flow to generate greater success with ease and to have more freedom and resource. Many of my clients have a similar complaint about being fed up with wasting so much of their life force working hard and want to have more time for living and to have a greater impact in the world. More and more of them began to ask me about this level of effortless flow they see me use that I've been able to create through this integration work and how to stabilize it and keep it going.

You have to have that aligned, resourced focus which is a stabilized, effortless Awake Alignment. This is different than concentrated focusing that we are taught growing up. Concentrated focus can be useful at times, but can also drain us. Nonstop concentrated focus is like pressing the gas pedal down nonstop on a Ferrari. Eventually, you can wear even that out. Many people get stuck in that loop powered by fear and lack and generally a lot of coffee and caffeine. Effortless Awake Alignment also requires relaxing into non-attachment, as you mentioned, with right doing and maintaining an easeful awake focus, or what I call a stabilized, effortless Awake Alignment in the core.

It generates a powerful field of energy, what you called your vortex, that is programmed with your stabilized alignment, programmed values with what you truly want. It's this vortex of energy that begins to build momentum on itself. It's almost like its own organic life form that begins to move forward in reality and grows, attracting to it all that it needs that is aligned to its vibration that we have total power over programming. As you aligned focus on this field with awareness and a resourced energy system, not stuck in contracted fear, it grows and grows and grows. It effortlessly attracts more and more of what you're looking for when you maintain that level of energy and operate in Presence while in a flow state.

I have also noticed from my own experience, when I'm being of service without any attachment, true authentic being of service, and true giving and being of true support, that the energy behind my field greatly amplifies. Everything seems to speed up naturally, effortlessly. True service can't be faked or mimicked from the mind. That is a true, authentic being of service that arises from the core of our being, not from ego desires.

What I've also realized is that when it comes to groups and working in flow with others, when many people get behind an intention, or multiple levels of synchronized intentions of being of service, they build a stable field that is held together by each being in the group. Some have named these morphogenetic fields. There's different kinds of fields everywhere, everything has a field, whether it's a human consciousness field, a bioenergetic field, everything from food to plant species generates a morphogenetic field that contains information giving off a frequency of vibration; they all maintain a field. And if you have an organization that is getting behind something with the intention to hold a field of intention from greater levels of mind with deeper levels of our being, things begin to open up naturally and effortlessly, things start to happen that can be viewed as supernatural.

Magical experiences start to happen that we can't fully explain, from synchronicities to experiences between group members having profound, powerful insights that might come from other realms of existence, wisdom that comes through, that these groups can start accessing while operating together in these flow states. When the field is held stable over time, the purpose or intention that we're holding as a group begins to manifest rapidly, and intentions are very powerful when we're holding that together as a group.

BILL: One of the things that I've played with is the idea of self-organizing systems. Our body is full of self-organizing systems. A single cell—it may be a heart cell that isn't working with all the other heart cells—has no value. A solitary cell can't function alone. It can only function as part of a group. Interestingly, you have all these different organs in the body, each one is a separate system, and each one isolated outside of the body has no real purpose. It's only when they're integrated together.

It's possible, at least we can hypothesize, that part of the evolution of life is not at the level of the physical only, because the physical is just one dimension, but at the higher emotional, energetic level, human beings are to some extent like single cells in a much more complex universal system. Certain individuals are naturally drawn to each other to perform functions that serve the whole. I wonder, in your experience of working with beings that are not just limited to this planet or dimension, if you've received any insights that there really is a grand design for the human species in terms of coming together in different ways to support a higher evolution of humanity.

ANDREW: From interactions I have had with beings, which I interpret as being from other realms or frequencies, it seems that there is a larger and deeper integration happening on a level beyond what I would call ordinary, everyday human consciousness; one could say there's something greater happening. Something greater is always happening. This time period is special. It's a monumental leap in consciousness that is exciting. If we look around the world, it's quite obvious that something wonderful is happening. It seems there's to be a drive toward a positive self-organization that is occurring within many individuals, generating new loving ways of being in the world that is naturally wanting to happen if we just get out of our own way and allow for the natural wisdom to be our guiding light to change.

As I learned to get out of my own way individually, a natural integration occurs where life easily works itself out, things start to show up naturally. All these problems I once had fell away with minimal external effort, and others are beginning to have this experience as well. As these individuals integrate, there is an attraction to each other. As groups now have come together, some are soul families returning back to each other and [they are] currently generating some powerful positive changes on this planet from an internal state of well-being combined with external aligned well-doing action.

These individuals have done some level of work within themselves; they understand that you have to be the change before change can occur. As greater integration occurs with the self, then groups come together and deepen integration and an intelligent self organization is starting to happen; not only at a human level—ordinary mind consciousness—but at all levels and dimensions of this universe. A great awakening is underway. It seems to be well beyond just the human realm. There are many people on this planet who have had contact with beings of all sorts; these are credible people who are normal everyday individuals, some from Ivy League schools, who are doing amazing things on this planet with credible backgrounds.

I've had conversations with some people who have ongoing communications with beings in other realms that seem to have loving intentions to support this positive organization occurring within humanity and to assist our planet during her own awakening. Not only on our planet, but other planets, there's something amazing happening in our galaxy, and in the universe, something really special seems to be occurring that we're all experiencing, some consciously and some unconsciously. If you choose to wake up to these experiences, you will not have to just blindly believe what you are reading. It's not just for one individual; it's for all of us to have.

I woke up to this interesting reality that there are many other beings, and they have contacted me, and some I don't pay any attention to and some I do. I'm very discerning who I let in, what I let in. I have developed ways to filter using my life navigation tools. I filter not only from the human level, but also from these other realms, and I would like to know what their intentions are. Many seem to be aligned to the greater good for the whole, knowing they are all connected to the whole, including the well-being of humanity as a whole and the planet.

We see that right now on the planet. There are many amazing things happening, but there are a lot of things that are about to unfold that could cause a lot of chaos and unnecessary pain on the planet if we all choose that timeline collectively. We need to organize from love, we need to come together not from fear and learn how to communicate as a collective race, and we need to do that at an accelerated rate right now to make real changes on the planet so that there is a planet for our children and others to live on and experience in this reality. If we do get out of our way, there is a loving wisdom that can guide us individually and as groups. The important thing is, we need to get out of our way, and that seems to be a complex challenge for many of us.

BILL: As a young boy growing up, my mother used to talk a lot about truth and beauty. Truth certainly seems to be in short supply on the planet recently. We have every kind of fake news going on and all these accusations and people saying, "Well, it doesn't matter whether it's true or not, it's just what people think is true and that's enough." Well, that may be enough on a very shallow level of existence, but there are universal truths. There are universal principles, and one of the observations that my mother made was that beauty exists. That there really is beauty in nature and in the universe, and if you have no other purpose that you can define for your existence, she would always suggest just be an emissary for beauty.

I think that's a useful fallback position because if everyone on the planet just focused on what their individual contribution to beauty can be—and it's manifested in many common ways, you know, "cleanliness is next to godliness" is an old saying. You go to the park, and if everything's in order, someone's created a beautiful park, and you have all the children laughing and playing and the parents enjoying, it creates a very high vibration. If you go to the park, and there's people who are inebriated and unkempt and the garden is not being kept, it doesn't create that high vibration. It creates a very negative vibration. So, there are many little things that each and every individual can do to contribute to a greater beauty and harmony within the universe. Interestingly, if we are all interconnected in these self-organizing systems, the impact of these little acts may be much, much greater than any of us can possibly perceive.

ANDREW: I feel that to be true. Your mom seems wise for teaching you this. At the deepest core of what I do is to get out of my own way as much as I can. Still I get in my way. When that happens, I have learned how to kindly let it go and shift back into Awake Alignment. I know deep down through my right actions that every time I orient toward love or wholeness and care that I know whatever I am doing ripples through the collective, it ripples through the universe, and it does have an impact on everything. Just like throwing a rock in a pond, you can see the ripples move all the way through the pond. It's how I feel about every action I take. It ripples through, whether that action is aligned or not. Whatever is powering the action depends on where it's coming from within our core. Is it ego action? Is it for the self? Is it selfish, or is it arising out of being, held stable in right alignment in service to the whole which lovingly includes our self?

BILL: Our wonderful friend and departed author Barbara Marx Hubbard spoke of conscious evolution. For Barbara, we were always evolving toward a higher and higher state of awareness in being. Whether true or not, it's a useful hypothesis because if we keep that as our focus, then we all do have a higher purpose that we can identify with, and that has immediate impact on our journeys as individuals.

When you're in the flow, you are likely to experience some of these higher states. I think we can end this book with the hope that everyone who's listening or reading this book will take a chance on themselves, forgive themselves for the moments when they're not in the flow. We all unfortunately, most of the time, we're not in the flow. But when you find yourself in the flow, cherish it and use it. Use it for good.

ANDREW: Life is always in flow, always in flux, it has always been waiting for you to arrive. When we align our systems in each moment to the flow of life, we are aligning to truth. Each one of us is a unique being with precious moments to be had, to be shared and be created. We don't have to externally work hard to receive what is already ours, what has always been ours. Just allow your system to become available through the work or whatever works for you.

The divine kingdom that is available to us all, it is here *Now*. Only when we are available to receive through orienting ourselves to Awake Alignment will we realize the abundant loving nature that has always been here. We can use any combination of tools currently available, like healing, self-reflection, coaching, mindfulness and whatever we find that works for our uniqueness, to support us in becoming available to receive life and to guide us into Awake Alignment. Once we arrive at the destination, all the tools and maps must be dropped to fully surrender into the moment for life to flow through us. Effort until effort is no longer required. Arrive and surrender into the arms of the infinite. All you have to do is show up for you and be available. Magic awaits. Life is a loving work of art in progress. We are that life. Never give it up.

Made in the USA
San Bernardino, CA
14 February 2020